P9-DIB-750

The Balkans 1815–1914

The Balkans 1815–1914

L. S. Stavrianos
Northwestern University

HOLT, RINEHART AND WINSTON, INC.
NEW YORK • CHICAGO • SAN FRANCISCO • ATLANTA • DALLAS
MONTREAL • TORONTO • LONDON • SYDNEY

Library of Congress Catalog Card Number: 63-12627
SBN: 03-082841-4
Printed in the United States of America
90123 68 987654321

Preface

The history of the Balkans in the nineteenth century is of more than regional significance for at least three reasons. First, and most obvious, is the impact of the Balkans on general European diplomacy. So pressing and persistent was the problem of what to do with the sultan's possessions in Southeastern Europe that the phrase "the Eastern Question" became a cliché with historians and journalists. During the period between 1815 and 1914 this "Eastern Question" twice plunged Europe into war, and on several other occasions dragged the European powers to the brink of conflict.

The nineteenth-century Balkans are significant also in providing a classic case study of the force of nationalism at work. It was during this century that the Balkan peoples made the transition from the age of theocracy to the age of nationalism. The complex combination of forces behind this transition helps explain the dynamics of one of the basic elements of modern history.

Finally, Balkan history in this period is noteworthy also in providing a fascinating example of the impact of the dynamic, industrialized West upon a static, agrarian society. This is part and parcel of the world-wide problem of the adjustment of backward areas to the Western industrial civilization that has enveloped the globe.

Further details and additional bibliographical references concerning the Balkan peninsula in the nineteenth-century are available in the author's *The Balkans Since 1453,* upon which this study is based.

January 1963 **L. S. STAVRIANOS**

Contents

CHAPTER . . . 1

The Land and the People

A visitor to the Balkan lands cannot help noticing about him countless signs of a long and varied past. In the course of his travels he is likely to encounter a Greek temple, a Roman bath, a Byzantine church, a Muslim mosque, or a Frankish castle. The variety in historical background reflected by these structures is explained in large part by the central location of the Balkan Peninsula. Jutting southward into the eastern Mediterranean, it constitutes an integral part of Europe. Yet at the same time it faces Asia across the narrow Aegean Sea, and its southern capes stretch down toward the coast of Africa.

The significance of this location at the crossroads of three continents is enhanced by the unusual accessibility of the Balkan lands. Unlike the Iberian and Apennine peninsulas, the Balkan Peninsula has no northern wall to shelter it from Central Europe. In place of the Alps and the Pyrenees there is the wide Danube River plain, which serves as a highway rather than a barrier. Likewise, to the west a mere fifty miles separate the heel of the Italian boot from the coast of Albania. In the south the island of Crete serves as a natural steppingstone between Greece and Egypt, while in the east the Aegean Islands serve a similar function between Greece and Asia Minor. This unusual accessibility from many directions has in large part determined Balkan history from the earliest times to the present. It explains why the Balkan Peninsula has traditionally been a battleground of peoples, empires, and cultures.

Almost as important as central location and accessibility is the mountainous terrain. In fact, the name "Balkan" is derived from the Turkish word for mountain. The only extensive plains are the Danubian in the north, the Macedonian and Thracian along the northern shore of the Aegean, and the Thessalian in Greece. On the western side of the peninsula are the Dinaric-Pindus ranges, a southern extension of the Alps. Similarly the Balkan Mountains, running east and west through central Bulgaria, are an extension of the Carpathians. To the south are the Rhodope Mountains, running in a southeasterly direction and gradually decreasing in altitude until they become low foothills when they reach the Aegean. This rugged and complex topography has profoundly influenced Balkan political development. It has prevented unification and encouraged isolation and particularism. Nowhere in the peninsula is there a natural center around which a great state might crystallize. Thus the normal political state of the Balkan Peninsula has been fragmentation. Unity in the past has not risen from within but has been forced from without by foreign conquerors, first the Romans and then the Turks.

The mountainous character of the Balkan Peninsula naturally has affected its river systems. Most rivers are short and of little value for navigation, for they shrink to shallow streams during the summer months and their mouths are blocked by silt carried down from the uplands. This is especially true along the Adriatic where the ranges run parallel to the coast. Here the rivers find their way to the sea only after many twists and turns, so that they are of little value and have played a negligible role in history. More important are the three rivers flowing south to the Aegean: the Maritsa, the Struma (Strymon), and the Vardar (Axios). The latter, with the great port of Saloniki near its mouth, forms the natural outlet for the Macedonian hinterland. By far the most outstanding of the Balkan rivers is the magnificent Danube with its numerous tributaries, particularly the Sava and the Morava. From prehistoric times it has served as a natural highway, linking the peninsula with Central Europe to the west and with the Eurasian steppes to the east. Countless waves of nomadic peoples have emerged from Central Asia, rounded the northern end of the Caspian Sea, swept along the shores of the Black Sea to the Danube valley, and then continued south to the Balkans or further up the valley to Central Europe.

For those who turned southward, a number of routes have pointed the way to the warm water and blue skies of the Mediterranean. At the northwestern tip of the peninsula, the Peartree Pass opens a passage southward to Trieste on the Adriatic. In the center of the Balkans, the Morava River offers a route from Belgrade to Nish and thence southward down the Vardar to Saloniki, or southeastward to Sofia and down the Maritsa to Edirne (Adrianople) and Istanbul (Constantinople). It is not surprising that Trieste, Saloniki, and Constantinople, the termini of the overland Balkan routes, traditionally have been contested by the maritime powers seeking to retain control of the Mediterranean, and by the land powers attempting to expand to the sea. Thus in the nineteenth century the Italians eyed Austrian-held Trieste, while the British were always ready to block Austrian economic designs on Saloniki or a Russian move to Constantinople.

In addition to location and terrain, the Balkans have been profoundly influenced by climate, of which there are two main types, the Mediterranean and the Continental. The Mediterranean prevails in southern Greece and in the two narrow coastal strips along the Aegean to Constantinople and along the Adriatic to Trieste. The remaining interior, which constitutes by far the larger proportion of the peninsula, is subject to the Continental climate. The distinguishing characteristic of the Mediterranean climate is the long, dry summer and cool winter with scattered rains. The tendency to aridity explains why the traditional Mediterranean products are olives, grapes, figs, and citrus fruits, rather than grain cereals, which require more regular rainfall. Likewise the lack of forests and grassy pastures means that the goat and the sheep in the Mediterranean areas take the place of the cow and the pig in the central Balkans. It is quite natural, therefore, that the tourist will be treated to roast suckling pig and plum brandy in Belgrade and to skewered lamb and wine in Athens.

The Continental climate differs from the Mediterranean in two respects: the winters are colder and longer, and the rainfall is more abundant and more evenly distributed through the year. This means that the central highlands, in contrast to the denuded mountains of the south, are covered with evergreen and deciduous forests. Likewise the valleys are sufficiently well watered to grow wheat, rye, oats, corn, flax, and other products typical of the whole of Central Europe.

Further north the broad Danubian plains of northern Yugoslavia and particularly of Rumania are reminiscent of the fertile Ukraine or of the American Midwest. Corn, oats, and especially wheat can be grown in such quantities that this region became the bread-basket of Western Europe in the nineteenth century, though in the twentieth it suffered severely from overseas competition.

As regards mineral resources, the most richly endowed country is Yugoslavia, with its copper, lead, zinc, bauxite, iron, chrome, antimony, gold, silver, and lignite. Rumania has noteworthy oil fields, by far the richest of the continent west of Russia. It should be noted, however, that during the nineteenth century these resources were but slightly exploited. Only a few deposits were worked, and these by foreign companies more interested in profits for shareholders than in sound economic development for the country concerned. Except for Rumania with her booming oil fields, none of the Balkan countries during this period were significantly affected by the exploitation of their mineral resources.

Turning from the land to the people, we find the peninsula populated by four main ethnic groups and several scattered minorities. The most numerous of the four groups are the South Slavs, who have settled in a great belt across the central Balkans from the Adriatic to the Black seas. These Slavs are divided into four subgroups: the Slovenes at the head of the Adriatic, the Croatians further to the southeast, the Serbians in the central Balkans around the Morava River, and the Bulgarians in the remaining territory to the Black Sea. The other three ethnic groups are the Rumanians to the north of the Slavs, and the Greeks and the Albanians to the south.

Reviewing briefly the circumstances in which these groups appeared in the Balkans, we note that in classical times the ancient Greeks inhabited the southern part of the peninsula, as their descendants do today, and that to the northwest and the northeast were two barbarian peoples, the Illyrians and the Thracians, respectively. The Illyrians originally inhabited most of present-day Yugoslavia but later were forced southward by the Slavic invaders. Thus today the descendants of these Illyrians, known as the Albanians, occupy only a small mountainous area along the southern Adriatic coast. The Thracians fared even worse at the hands of the Slavs. They were so effectively dispersed or absorbed that only a few survivors remain today. These are known as the Vlachs, a wild and largely nomadic group of shepherds and cattle breeders who are to be found scattered in mountainous areas throughout the peninsula. Their total number at the end of the nineteenth century has been estimated at 140,000. Since then they have steadily dwindled because of assimilation with their sedentary neighbors.

The next people to appear were the Rumanians, the descendants of the early Dacians, who were subjected to Roman rule from A.D. 107 to 274. During this period they were Romanized to a considerable degree, intermarrying with their conquerors and adopting their language. Hence the origin of the term "Rumanian" and the basically Latin character of the modern Rumanian language.

The most radical change in the ethnic composition of the peninsula occurred in the sixth and seventh centuries with the invasions of Slavic tribes originating in the low-lying areas north of the Carpathians. By sheer weight of numbers they pushed back or assimilated the Illyrians and Thracians, and at times even menaced the East Roman or Byzantine Empire with its capital at Constantinople. As noted earlier, these newcomers gradually settled down in the central Balkans and developed into the separate Slovenian, Croatian, and Serbian peoples. Toward the end of the seventh century some of these Slavs were conquered in turn by the Bulgarians, an Asiatic people related to the earlier Huns. The Bulgarians, however, were few in number and soon were so completely assimilated by their subjects that only their name persists to the present. The modern Bulgarians, therefore, are considered one of the South Slavic subgroups, and are, in fact, completely Slavic in language, general culture, and physical appearance.

In this manner the peninsula acquired its basic ethnic pattern over one thousand years ago. Since then several minority groups have appeared in varying circumstances. The Ottoman Turkish domination of the Balkans from the fifteenth to the early twentieth centuries led to a scattering of isolated Turkish ethnic islands. With the recession of their empire, most of these Turks returned to their homeland, so that insignificant remnants are left in the peninsula today. The only exception is to be found in the area immediately to the west of Constantinople. This area, known as Eastern or Turkish Thrace, is the only part of the peninsula remaining to the Turks, and its population of about half a million, or one and a quarter million if Istanbul is included, is almost entirely Turkish. Balkan ethnography was further complicated by the practice of the Austrian government of deliberately planting colonies along their frontiers as a defense against the enemy. Thus they settled Germans along the Danube, so that prior to World War II Rumania had a German minority of about 750,000 and Yugoslavia had about 500,000. Finally, it should be noted that until World War II, about 1,000,000 Jews were living in Rumania, where they had migrated from Russia and Poland in the seventeenth and eighteenth centuries. Approximately another 170,000 were scattered in Bulgaria, Yugoslavia, and Greece, most of these being descendants of sixteenth century refugees from Spain and Portugal, who were given asylum by the Turks.

Turning to religious affiliations today, the Balkan peoples are predominantly Orthodox Christians. The main exceptions are the Roman Catholics in the west and the scattered Muslims who are a by-product of the centuries of Turkish rule. More specifically, Yugoslavia is about 50 percent Orthodox (mostly Serbs), 33 percent Roman Catholic (Croatians, Slovenes, and Italians), and 12 percent Muslim, the remaining 5 percent being Protestants, Jews, and Greek Catholics. Rumania is 81 percent Orthodox, 9 percent Greek Catholic, 7 percent Roman Catholic and 3 percent Jewish, Protestant, and Muslim. Finally, Albania is unique in Europe with 70 percent of her population being Muslim, 20 percent Orthodox, and 10 percent Catholic.

In conclusion, there arises the question why four major ethnic strains and several minor ones have persisted in an area not quite the size of Texas. The geographical factors noted above provide a partial explanation: the location and accessibility of the peninsula that led to repeated invasions, and the mountainous terrain that promoted compartmentalization rather than unification. It should not be assumed, however, that there are more ethnic strains in the Balkans than in Western Europe. If we look behind the façade of national unity in France, we find Iberian, Ligurian, Frankish, Norman, and Gallic strains. Likewise in Germany there are Slavic, Celtic, Baltic, and Teutonic elements; and in England there are Celtic, Anglo-Saxon, Scandinavian, and Norman ones.

The difference between the Balkans and the West, then, is not in the number of component ethnic elements but rather in the particular circumstances that made possible the unification of several such strains into a national unit in the one case and prevented such unification in the other. In medieval times the inhabitants of present-day England, France, and Germany by no means felt themselves to be English, French, and German. Their loyalties were regional rather than national, and it was not until recent times that the nation-state used modern techniques for mass indoctrination and assimilation to stimulate a sense of national consciousness. The Balkan peoples, by contrast, were ruled not by assimilative nation-states but rather by the multinational Hapsburg and Ottoman empires. These agglomerations, as we shall note below, lacked the technological and institutional facilities for integrating and unifying their subjects, with the results that Greeks, Slavs, Rumanians, and Albanians all retained their individual identities and eventually won independence and formed separate states.

Thus the unique feature of Balkan ethnic evolution is that virtually all the peoples that have actually settled there in the past, as distinguished from those that have simply marched through, have been able to preserve their identity to the present. The significance of this may be illustrated by imagining a Balkan type of ethnic development in England. Had that occurred we would meet, in a journey through England today, Britons speaking Welsh, Romans speaking Latin, Angles and Saxons speaking their Germanic dialects, Scandinavians speaking Danish, and Normans speaking Old French. Furthermore, some of these peoples might have maintained separate state structures, such as an independent Scotland and an independent Wales.

In a British setting such a situation seems fantastic. And yet this preservation of ethnic groups through the centuries is precisely what has happened in the Balkans. This is one of the unique and fundamental factors that has influenced the historical development of the peninsula to the present.

CHAPTER . . . 2

Awakening of the Nationalities 1815–1856

At the beginning of the nineteenth century the Balkan peoples entered a new phase of their history, a phase whose distinguishing characteristic was their awakening national consciousness. This awakening is taken for granted as a belated repetition of what had occurred earlier in Western Europe. Yet the question remains why it took place at that particular period rather than at some other during the three to four centuries of Turkish rule. To answer this question it is necessary to understand the complex of historical forces operating in the Balkans in the nineteenth century—a complex comprising the continued decline of the Ottoman Empire and the increasing interests and interventions of the great powers, as well as the awakening of the Balkan peoples. These forces did not operate independently of each other. Indeed, nineteenth-century Balkan history is the history of the interplay of these three trends, with now one playing the more prominent role and now the other. In this chapter we shall first analyze these trends in order to understand the dynamics of nineteenth-century Balkan politics, and then trace the course of politics to 1856.

Dynamics of Nineteenth-Century Balkan Politics

Viewed externally, the Ottoman Empire in the early nineteenth century was still a great power. In North Africa it extended from Algiers to Egypt; in the Middle East it embraced Arabia, the Levant states, Mesopotamia, and Asia Minor; while in Europe it included the entire Balkan Peninsula north to the Danube and east to the river Pruth. This façade of empire was impressive, but the substance behind the façade was fragile and crumbling. The powerful and glittering empire of Suleiman the Magnificent (1520–1566) had long since passed. The vigorous Ottoman dynasty was now degenerate, the imperial economy stagnant, the formerly efficient bureaucracy corrupted, and the armed forces demoralized and impotent. The empire had become an empty shell, especially in comparison with a burgeoning Western Europe that had been transformed by the Renaissance, the overseas expansion, the Commercial and Industrial revolutions, and scientific and military advances.

Typical of the disintegration of Ottoman rule was the situation in the Balkans, where the Ionian Islands had passed under British rule and the Moldavian and Wallachian principalities across the Danube had become virtual Russian protectorates. In other regions, such as

Serbia and the island of Crete, the *de facto* rulers were the janissaries, formerly crack imperial troops that had degenerated into an extortionist praetorian guard. Almost the only exceptions to the prevailing chaos and misgovernment were in southern Albania and northern Bulgaria, which were ruled ruthlessly but firmly by Ali Pasha and Osman Pasvan-Oglu respectively. Both men started out as brigands and gradually carved out personal domains by virtue of their abilities and unscrupulous exploitation of every opportunity. In both cases the imperial government attempted to check these powerful potentates but, finding this to be beyond its resources, ended by recognizing their authority. The result was a rough and ready type of personal rule that at least protected their grateful subjects from the extortions of janissaries and tax collectors.

In conclusion, the Ottoman government in the early nineteenth century was a government in little more than name. This was strikingly demonstrated when Sultan Selim III attempted to revitalize the empire by imitating the West rather than by trying to return to the days of Suleiman. His plans included the reorganization of administration, the revamping of education, and the establishment of a modern Western-type army. The latter proposal was violently opposed by the janissaries, who naturally feared a rival armed force. They were supported by the ulema or religious leaders, who regarded as sacrilegious any borrowing whatsoever from the Christian infidels. The combination of these military and religious vested interests proved too much for the unfortunate Selim, who was strangled in 1808 by the mutineers. This failure to reform the empire was immensely significant, for it stimulated the other two historical trends of this period, the intrusion of the great powers and the awakening of the subject nationalities.

The relations of the European powers with the Ottoman Empire were very different in the nineteenth century from the earlier days when Turkish armies twice besieged Vienna. The turning point came with the Karlowitz treaty (1699) by which the Turks were forced to surrender their large trans-Danubian holdings to the Hapsburgs. Never again was Europe threatened by the star and crescent, which for almost three centuries had menaced its security. Instead Europe now faced precisely the opposite problem—how to fill the political vacuum created in the Near East by the rapidly declining Ottoman power.

Austria and Russia were the first to take advantage of the weakened Turks. By the beginning of the nineteenth century they had conquered the vast territories across the Danube and along the northern shore of the Black Sea. During most of this period Britain had been quite unconcerned by the Russian advance, partly because she was then in the midst of her prolonged struggle with France, but also because she was carrying on a highly profitable trade with Russia. In the course of the nineteenth century this commercial and political situation changed and British policy changed with it. Anglo-Russian trade declined while Anglo-Turkish trade forged far ahead. At the same time Britain and Russia clashed during the political scramble following Napoleon's downfall, particularly over the question of Poland's fate. For the first time the Foreign Office came to regard further Russian expansion in the Near East as incompatible with British imperial interests. Specifically, it feared that Russian control of the Straits would endanger Britain's profitable trade with Turkey, her naval power in the Mediterranean, and her position in India. Thus British diplomacy shifted sharply and strove throughout the nineteenth century to preserve the integrity of the Ottoman Empire.

Britain's policy of *status quo* conflicted with the more dynamic aims of the three other great powers that were particularly interested in the Balkans: Russia, France, and Austria. Of these three, Russia, with her aspirations for Constantinople and the Straits, was the most persistent opponent of Britain. After her spectacular territorial gains under Catherine and Alexander, Russia was not likely to halt her advance abruptly at the Dniester River. It is an oversimplification, however, to assert that Russia invariably strove to dismember the sultan's domains. We shall see that in 1829 she halted her armies outside Constantinople and deliberately decided to accept the existence of the moribund Ottoman Empire. Likewise, in the 1830s she cooperated with Britain in supporting the sultan against the overly ambitious Mehemet Ali of Egypt. Despite these exceptions it remains true that Russian diplomacy was generally anti-Turkish while British diplomacy was usually pro-Turkish. Hence the frequent crises and periodic wars of the nineteenth century.

France also was vitally interested in Balkan and Near Eastern affairs. At one time her influence in the Ottoman court had been unrivaled. In 1535 she was the first Christian power to conclude an alliance and a commercial agreement with the Turks. From then on her diplomats worked unceasingly to bolster the Ottoman Empire, because it was to the advantage of France to have a strong Turkish ally on Austria's rear. Napoleon's erratic diplomacy, however, undermined French influence in Constantinople. Furthermore, defeated France was forced to yield both Malta and the Ionian Islands to Britain. Thus France's position in the Near East in 1815 was at an all-time low. It is not surprising that in the 1830s she sought to advance her position by supporting the insurgent Mehemet Ali of Egypt against the

Constantinople government. But this strategy failed in the face of combined Anglo-Russian opposition. During the following decades France usually ranged herself on the side of Britain. The explanation is not that the two powers had no differences, but that they had an overriding common interest in blocking Russian expansion. Thus Britain and France fought together against Russia during the Crimean War and continued to cooperate on most crucial issues until World War I.

The other major power interested in the Balkans in the nineteenth century was Austria. After her great triumph in the Karlowitz settlement, she alternated between two contradictory policies toward the ancient Turkish foe. Sometimes she attacked him as a weak neighbor ripe for partition; at other times she supported him as a useful bulwark against the menacing advance of Russia. During the eighteenth century Austria followed both these policies at various times. Then in 1815 she acquired Dalmatia and other former Venetian possessions, which made her the dominant power in the Adriatic and in the western Balkans. During the rest of the nineteenth century Austria usually was on the side of Britain supporting the *status quo* in the Near East. She feared that a major rearrangement would primarily strengthen Russia, whom she considered particularly dangerous because of the many Slavic subjects in the Hapsburg empire who might be attracted by Russian national and religious propaganda.

In conclusion, these four powers—Britain, Russia, France, and Austria—were the ones most involved in Balkan affairs during the nineteenth century. They determined to a considerable degree the course of events throughout the Near Eastern world. Their conflicting interests and policies explain in large part why the moribund Ottoman Empire was able to survive until

World War I despite its miserable showing against the Greek revolutionaries and Mehemet Ali in the opening decades of the nineteenth century.

It should be added that Italy and Germany also participated in Balkan affairs following their unification by 1871. The granting of the Berlin–Bagdad Railway contract to a German group in 1903 and the Italian seizure of Tripolitania and of the Dodecanese Islands in 1911–1912 are symptomatic of the appearance of these two powers in the eastern Mediterranean. It was not until the turn of the century, however, that they began directly and appreciably to affect the course of events in the Balkans.

Turning finally to the awakening of the Balkan peoples, we have noted that this was promoted by the feebleness of the Turks and by the roles of the great powers. Equally important, however, was the effect of certain developments within the peninsula which transformed the static and theocratic Balkan society of the early Ottoman period. During the centuries after the fall of Byzantium the Orthodox Church dominated education, written literature, and intellectual life in general. The Balkan world during this early period was a nonnational Orthodox world, and the subjects of the sultan thought of themselves as Orthodox Christians rather than as Slavs or Greeks or Rumanians. National policies and national objectives were virtually nonexistent. Gradually, however, this Orthodox hegemony was undermined, and the age of theocracy gave way to the age of nationalism.

One reason for this transition was the rapid growth in the volume of trade during the eighteenth century. Corn and cotton were grown in the Balkan plains and exported to meet the rising demand of Western cities for foodstuffs and of Western industries for cotton. This trade in turn led to the appearance of a new class of merchants, artisans, and mariners who had a very different attitude towards the West from that of the hitherto dominant Orthodox prelates. Some of these new elements had visited Western cities in the course of their commercial operations, and in many cases lived permanently abroad. They usually had been favorably impressed by what they had observed—the political institutions, the rule of law, the economic prosperity, and the intellectual life. While the Orthodox churchmen had branded Western civilization as "Latin" and therefore heretical and repugnant, the new middle class viewed it as a model to be imitated. The churchmen had dismissed Western scientists as *antitheoi,* or antitheists, and their teachings as *morosophia,* or foolish wisdom. By contrast the pioneer Greek nationalist, Adamantios Korais, referred repeatedly to *photismene,* or "enlightened," Europe.

The Balkan merchant class eagerly sought to bring Europe's Enlightenment to their enslaved and benighted countrymen back home. The Serbian merchants in southern Hungary, the Bulgarian merchants in southern Russia and the Danubian Principalities, and the Greek merchants scattered widely in foreign cities such as Trieste, Venice, Vienna, Budapest, Bucharest, and Odessa, all contributed greatly to the awakening of their respective countries. They did so by shipping home books and equipment, by sending young fellow countryment to foreign universities, and by financing the publication of books and newspapers in their native languages, including the translation of works by Voltaire, Locke, Rousseau, Leibnitz, and others.

These economic and intellectual developments inevitably had political repercussions. The merchants who consciously spread the ideas of the Enlightenment were likely also to support movements for political liberation. It is not mere coincidence that, as we shall see, Greek merchants organized the revolutionary Philike Hetairia; pig dealers were prominent in the Serbian revolt; and craft guilds sparked the Bulgarian national revival.

These revolutionary leaders were provided with mass support because of a change in land tenure that aroused the hitherto inert peasantry. When the Turks conquered the Balkans they divided the choicest lands into nonheritable fiefs or timars. The holders of these timars were usually deserving Turkish military leaders, who were granted only the right to collect certain specified revenues from their fiefs, a right that was revokable if they failed to perform their stipulated military duties. By contrast the peasants on the timars were assured the right to till hereditary plots so long as they paid a defined and customary tithe. In the eighteenth century, however, the timars gave way to the much more onerous chifliks, a shift for which the growing market for corn and cotton in the West was responsible. So long as the timar system prevailed, no substantial surplus could be accumulated for export. Accordingly, the landlords took advantage of the weakness of the imperial government to violate the two regulations that stood in the way of profit: the nonheritable nature of their fiefs and the legal limits on the peasant obligations. The landlords increased levies at will and evicted peasants who refused to meet their demands. The formerly free cultivators were suppressed to virtual serfdom, and the way was cleared for the uncontrolled exploitation of the peasantry for the production of export commodities. In this manner the timars were transformed into chifliks. The political implication of this development is evident; it was the chifliks that were largely responsible for the mass peasant support behind the nineteenth-century uprisings.

This combination of economic, intellectual, and political developments made the Balkan peoples susceptible to Europe's ideologies and revolutions. The English and American revolutions were too remote to exert much influence, but the French Revolution, and Napoleon's exploits, struck a responsive chord in the new Balkans. This is apparent in the following testimony by a contemporary Greek revolutionary:

> The French Revolution in general awakened the minds of all men. . . . All the Christians of the Near East prayed to God that France should wage war against the Turks, and they believed that they would be freed. . . . But when Napoleon made no move, they began to take measures for freeing themselves.[1]

The Serbian Revolt

The first Balkan people to take up arms against the Turks were the Serbs. The origins and course of their uprising illustrate clearly the operation of the historical forces considered above. The revolt began because of the breakdown of Ottoman administration. In ordinary times the Serbian peasants had enjoyed a well-developed system of self-government in their villages. They had virtually no contact with the sultan's officials in Belgrade and their tax load was light. They paid a small head tax for the imperial treasury, and a levy of one tenth of their grain crop for the Turkish landlords or spahis. Furthermore, the peasants were free to move, so that the spahis found it expedient to treat them fairly.

When the Serbs rose in revolt in 1804 they did so not [illegible] of this governmental system but rather because of its disintegration. An early symptom was the rise of

[1] Ch. Photios [Chrysanthopoulos], *Apomnemoneumata peri tes Hellenikes epanastaseos* [Memoirs of the Greek Revolution] (Athens, 1899), I. 1.

chifliks, which alienated the peasantry in Serbia as elsewhere. Another was the lawlessness of the janissaries, who openly defied the pasha in Belgrade who was the sultan's representative. The janissaries victimized even the spahis, forcibly seizing their chifliks and exploiting the Serb tenants even more ruthlessly than customary. The reform-minded sultan, Selim III, tried to remedy the situation by sending out enlightened and vigorous pashas. One of these, Hadji Mustafa, went so far as to arm the Serbs, but in the end he, like his master, was slain by the unruly praetorians. There now followed a reign of terror and bloodshed. The Serbs appealed to Constantinople, and when this brought no relief they finally took up arms in desperation. Thus the uprising at the outset was not a revolutionary affair directed against Ottoman rule. The Serbs wanted not a new order, but a return to the old order with its autonomy and security.

The head of the revolt was Karageorge, a prosperous hog dealer who had military experience because of earlier service under the Austrians. He proved to be a first-rate commander, and in addition, he received substantial aid from fellow Serbs across the Danube under Hapsburg rule. Thus Karageorge was able to defeat three Turkish armies, and by December 1806 he had captured Belgrade itself.

At this point the great powers appeared upon the scene and, henceforth, determined in large degree the course of events. Sultan Selim had decided late in 1806 to intervene in the European war that was raging, and threw in his lot with Napoleon. Immediately he was attacked on land by Russia and on sea by Britain. Selim naturally wished to be rid of the Serbian distraction, so he offered to meet Karageorge's demand for an autonomous Serbia within the Ottoman framework. But at the same time the Russians offered money and arms to the

Serbs if they continued fighting against the Turks. Karageorge had to choose between autonomy under the sultan and cooperation with the tsar. He chose the latter, and thereby changed the character of the Serb uprising. What had begun as a protest against janissary oppression now became a full-fledged war for independence.

Karageorge soon regretted the choice he had made. The Serbian-Russian alliance was signed on July 10, 1807. Three days earlier Tsar Alexander had suddenly switched sides and concluded the Tilsit Treaty with Napoleon. Since the Turks were Napoleon's allies, Alexander signed an armistice with them the following month. Thus the Serbs were left alone to face their enemy. For several years they had a reprieve because the Turks and the Russians could not agree on final peace terms and continued hostilities in a desultory fashion. But the final blow for the Serbs came in 1812 when the tsar hastily signed the Bucharest Treaty with the Turks in order to face the impending onslaught by Napoleon's Grand Army. For the next few years the Russians were locked in mortal combat with the French invaders. The Turks now could throw all their forces against the presumptuous Serbs. They attacked from three sides, and by the end of 1813 had retaken Belgrade.

The victorious Turks exacted bloody revenge with wholesale massacres. They seized lands which they had never before held, and planted garrisons of unruly janissaries all over the country. The terror and spoliation were so extreme that another revolt broke out on Palm Sunday, 1815. The leader was Milosh Obrenovich, who had risen to prominence after Karageorge fled across the Danube following his defeat. Milosh had tried earnestly to collaborate with the returning Turks, but finally was forced to give up the attempt as hopeless. When he finally resorted to arms, the international situation was much more favorable than it had been for Karageorge. By June 1815 Napoleon had suffered final defeat at Waterloo and had been shipped off to St. Helena. Now Russia was free to turn to the Balkans, and the Turks accordingly were anxious to reach a quick settlement with the Serbs. Milosh, being more of a diplomat than a warrior, was ready to accept modest concessions and to wait for opportunities to extract more. A compromise was reached in December 1815 by which Milosh was recognized as supreme knez or lord of the pashalik, and the Serbs were to retain their arms and to hold a national skupshtina or assembly. But the Ottoman administrators and garrisons were to remain as before, and taxes and tribute were to continue to be sent to Constantinople. Thus the twelve-year struggle ended with Serbia recognized as an autonomous principality under Ottoman suzerainty.

The new principality, it should be noted, was restricted in area, comprising roughly the region bounded by the Danube and Sava rivers in the north, the Drina River in the west, and Bulgaria in the east. This state was ruled until 1839 by Milosh Obrenovich, and then until 1842 by his son Milan. The latter was ousted in favor of Alexander Karageorgevich, a son of the great Karageorge who had led the Serbs in 1804. During the following decades these two dynasties, the Obrenovich and the Karageorgevich, succeeded one another as the rulers of Serbia, and later of Yugoslavia, until the coming of the Communists during World War II.

The Greek War of Independence

The revolt of the Greeks in 1821 followed that of the Serbs in time but not in importance. The Greek uprising was a much more significant affair for Europe as well as for the Balkans. The strategic location of the

Greek lands in the eastern Mediterranean brought the great powers into sharp and open conflict. Also, the Ottoman Empire as a whole was jarred by the Greek revolt because of the key position of Greek administrators and prelates in the imperial structure.

Most Greeks, like other Balkan Christians, were simple peasants living quietly in their villages. A small minority, however, was so extraordinarily active and highly placed that the group was almost as influential in the Ottoman Empire as the Turks themselves. This minority of influential Greeks became important in the seventeenth century when the Turks, no longer winning easy victories against the West, had to establish normal diplomatic relations and to negotiate with the European powers. Lacking the necessary linguistic and diplomatic skills, they employed the so-called Phanariotes as secretaries and interpreters.

The term "Phanariote" is derived from the lighthouse or Phanar district of Constantinople, where the Orthodox patriarch established his headquarters following the loss of St. Sophia to the Turks in 1453. Gradually Greek merchants as well as clergymen settled in this district. These merchants, or Phanariotes, prospered greatly as imperial tax farmers, purveyors to the court, contractors for imperial projects, and international traders. These activities gave them first-hand knowledge of Western customs and languages, and for this reason they began to be employed in the Ottoman bureaucracy. Gradually they rose to the topmost ranks as "dragomans" of various departments or ministries. The title meant literally "interpreters," but in practice dragomans functioned as undersecretaries and frequently were the key figures behind the scenes. From 1711 onward, Phanariotes also served as governors of the Moldavian and Wallachian principalities with the title of hospodars or princes. In addition, the Phanariotes infiltrated the administrative offices of the Constantinople patriarchate. This was of more than local significance, for it meant that in most of the Balkan lands they managed church properties and revenues, supervised the monasteries, and safeguarded the valuable liturgical objects. Only strictly ecclesiastical affairs were left to the clergy; the other functions were appropriated by the ubiquitous Phanariotes.

Meanwhile the great bulk of the Greek people remained politically inert peasants, at least during the early centuries of Ottoman rule. So long as they paid the customary taxes, they were left pretty much alone by their Turkish overlords. With the eventual deterioration of Ottoman rule the Greek peasantry, like the Serbian, was adversely affected. The onerous chiflik system spread over the fertile plains areas. It is estimated that by the beginning of the nineteenth century the 40,000 Turks who lived in the Peloponnesus owned 3,000,000 stremmata of good land (a stremma being roughly equal to a quarter of an acre), while the 360,000 Greeks were left with only 1,500,000 stremmata. Thus, on a per capita basis, the Turks had eighteen times as much land as the Greeks. Furthermore, most of the lands left to the Greeks was in the hands of a local oligarchy known as the primates or kodjabashis. Most of the peasants, then, had the choice of working as laborers for either Turkish or Greek landowners. It is not surprising that the Peloponnesus was to become the center of the Greek revolution. It should also be noted that the more daring and militant of these disaffected peasants took to the mountains and became outlaws. These klephts, as they were called, captured the national imagination with daring exploits that were endlessly related in popular folklore.

Greece had not only a discontented peasantry and outlaw bands, but also a rapidly growing merchant class that found Ottoman rule increasingly intolerable.

The Massacre at Scio, painting by Eugène Delacroix depicting a scene during the Greek War of Independence. *(Louvre, Paris; Giraudon)*

A number of developments contributed to the extraordinary growth of commerce in the Greek lands in the eighteenth century. One was the conclusion of the Karlowitz Treaty in 1699, which made possible the resumption of trade with Venice and the Austrian Empire. Another was Russia's expansion to the Black Sea by the treaties of Kuchuk Kainarji (1774) and Jassy (1792). Certain provisions of these treaties allowed Greek merchants to trade in the Black Sea, which hitherto had been closed to Christian shipping. They quickly took advantage of the opportunity to sell Greek fruits, wine, and olive oil in return for Russian wheat. Then during the French Revolutionary and Napoleonic Wars, the British and the French virtually destroyed each other's merchant marine in the Mediterranean. The enterprising Greeks stepped into the vacuum and gained control of most of the Mediterranean shipping trade. By 1813 the Greek merchant marine had risen to 615 ships totalling 153,580 tons, manned by 37,526 seamen and equipped with 5878 cannon. The cannon, which were to prove useful when the revolution began, were standard equipment for merchant ships in the Mediterranean because of the Barbary pirates.

This economic upsurge led to the appearance of a new middle class, both in the Greek lands and in the Greek mercantile communities abroad. The more numerous and the more wealthy this class became, the more intolerable it found the inefficiency and rapacity of Ottoman officials. It is not surprising that it was Greek merchants in Odessa who founded in 1814 the revolutionary secret organization, Philike Hetairia or Society of Friends. It should not be imagined that all elements in Greek society immediately rallied behind the Hetairia. Individual exceptions aside, the merchants and chiflik peasants were ready to take up arms, while the Phanariotes, the top Orthodox clergy, and the primates were lukewarm or openly hostile. When the revolt began in 1821, the Peloponnesian primates were persuaded to join only after being assured by the Hetairia, quite unjustifiably, that Russia was behind the undertaking.

During the first year of fighting the Greek revolutionaries won control of the Peloponnesus and various Aegean islands. By the summer of 1822 they extended their operations north of the Isthmus of Corinth, capturing Athens and Thebes. But now the insurrection found its limits, for in the north the Turks had crushed the outbreaks in Thessaly and Macedonia. During the following years the two sides were locked in stalemate. The Turks were too inefficient to mobilize their superior resources effectively, while the Greeks were hopelessly divided on both regional and class lines. Primates were ranged against peasants, prelates against village priests, shipowners against sailors, and Peloponnesians against continentals and against islanders. By 1823 two rival Greek governments existed, and in the next year there was open civil war between them.

The deadlock between the Greeks and the Turks was ended in 1825 by outside intervention, first by the Egyptains, who tipped the scales in favor of the Turks, and then by the European powers, who rescued the Greeks and finally won for them complete independence. Mehemet Ali of Egypt intervened in the Greek war only after Sultan Mahmud had accepted his conditions. He was to receive the pashalik of Crete, and his son Ibrahim was to become governor of the reconquered Peloponnesus. Thanks to the indiscipline of the Greek sailors, whose pay was in arrears, Ibrahim was able to conquer Crete and then to land his army in the Peloponnesus. The Egyptian troops were modern-trained, bayonet-wielding regulars who easily scattered the Greek guerrillas. Within a year they had overrun the Peloponnesus, while the Turks recaptured Athens.

At this point, when the revolution appeared doomed, the situation changed overnight with the intervention of the European powers. Initially they had all opposed the uprising, not because they had any illusions concerning the decrepit Ottoman Empire, but rather because they opposed revolution on principle, and also because they could not agree on what should take the place of the empire. They preferred to bolster the tottering imperial structure rather than to risk the dangers of partitioning. This strategy failed because the insurrection did not, as Metternich expected, "burn itself out beyond the pale of civilization." Rather it blazed on, and the longer it remained aflame, the more European public opinion rallied to the side of the Greeks. The latter were regarded as Christians fighting Muslims, and as the descendants of Pericles and Aristotle struggling against Turkish barbarism. The mounting philhellenic movement was especially strong in Russia, where there was the added appeal of the Orthodox religious bond with the Greeks. Finally the British foreign minister, George Canning, decided on joint intervention to forestall the danger of unilateral Russian action.

On April 4, 1826 Britain and Russia signed the St. Petersburg Protocol in which they agreed to mediate with the aim of establishing an autonomous Greece under Ottoman suzerainty. The desperate Greeks quickly accepted the mediation proposal, but the Turks and Egyptians were naturally reluctant with victory in sight. Canning therefore prepared for action by negotiating the Treaty of London (July 6, 1827) with France and Russia. This provided that the Allies should again offer mediation, and if the sultan rejected it they would "exert all the means which circumstances may suggest" to force the cessation of hostilities. The following month the Greeks again accepted mediation and the Turks again refused. The powers accordingly sent their fleets to intercept Ibrahim's supply ships. In the process shots were exchanged, and the final outcome was the complete destruction of a Turko-Egyptian fleet at Navarino Bay (October 20, 1827).

The Greek question was still far from settlement because of the unexpected death of Canning shortly before Navarino. His successor, the Duke of Wellington, publicly deplored Navarino as an "untoward event" and made clear his intention of protecting Turkish integrity against the Russians. But no other course could have been more nicely calculated to defeat this object. Sultan Mahmud was emboldened by Wellington's support to continue hostilities in Greece, so Russia declared war in April 1828. This unilateral action was precisely what Canning had successfully sought to avoid during the preceding years.

After being unexpectedly stalled by Turkish fortresses on the southern bank of the Danube, the Russians finally broke through, crossed the Balkan Mountains, and entered Adrianople in August 1829. Russian cannon now could be heard in Constantinople. The decrepit Ottoman Empire at last appeared to be approaching its end. At this critical point the Russian government decided against Ottoman partition for two reasons: it would create a "labyrinth of difficulties and complications" with the other powers, and Russia "would be called on to meet dangerous enemies in southern Europe instead of indifferent Turks." This policy in favor of the *status quo* was followed by Russia during the following decades when, as we shall note, she supported the sultan against Egypt's Mehemet Ali.

For the time being, Russia ended the war with Turkey by accepting the very moderate Treaty of Adrianople (September 14, 1829). She gave up her conquests in the Balkans, and in return she advanced her frontier from the northern to the southern mouth of the Danube and gained certain additional privileges in the Danubian Principalities. The Turks also agreed to accept the decision of the great powers with respect to Greece.

On February 3, 1830 the powers concluded the London Protocol declaring Greece an independent and monarchical state under the guarantee of the three Allied powers. On British insistence, the northern frontier of Greece was drawn from the Gulf of Arta in the west to the Gulf of Volo in the east, leaving little more than the Peloponnesus and the Cyclades Islands. This meant a population of about 800,000 in the new kingdom, as against three times that number of Greeks in the Turkish provinces and in the British-held Ionian Islands. Thus, thanks to British fears that Greece would come under Russian influence, the country was born a rump state. Throughout the nineteenth century its energies were to be spent in pursuit of the irredentist goal—the redemption of the compatriots under foreign rule.

Finally it should be noted that the powers that had made possible the creation of an independent Greece also selected a foreign ruler for the new state. This was Prince Otho of Bavaria, who remained on the throne from 1833 to 1862. He was then unseated by a popular uprising, and was succeeded by Prince William George of the Danish Glücksberg dynasty. Despite repeated revolutions and periodic exiles, this dynasty managed to return to power following the second World War.

Ottoman Reform and Near Eastern Crises

The decades following the Greek War of Independence witnessed two important developments in the Near East: the Ottoman reform movement begun by Sultan Mahmud II, and the European-wide crises precipitated by the expansionism of Mehemet Ali of Egypt. Neither of these developments was strictly Balkan in origin and in scope. Yet both did affect the Balkans indirectly, and both provide the background necessary for understanding the Crimean War that followed. For these reasons, the Ottoman reforms and the Near Eastern crises of the 1830s and 1840s will now be briefly surveyed.

The first successful Ottoman reformer was Mahmud II who came to the throne in 1808. The prospects for reform seemed hopeless at the time, for Selim III had just been murdered by the janissaries and their allies. Yet Mahmud accomplished much during his reign, and stands out as the great reforming sultan of his dynasty. His major achievement was the destruction of the janissary corps which had been the greatest obstacle to change. The janissaries had been thoroughly discredited by their miserable showing against a relative handful of Greek guerrillas. Mahmud, who was a more practical man than Selim, made careful preparations for the showdown. He won over the ulema or religious leaders by promotions and favors, and placed dependable men in key positions. Then he proposed his plan for modernizing the army by adopting new weapons, Western-type drill, and common uniforms. On the night of June 14, 1826, the janissaries overturned their soup kettles, the customary sign of revolt. But this time they met their nemesis. A large body of reliable troops were brought into the city, and the janissaries, deserted by the ulema and the populace, were all either slaughtered or exiled to outlying provinces.

Mahmud at last was the unchallenged master of his realm. First he proceeded with the organization of a new and modern army. Then, with a zeal reminiscent of Peter the Great, he built bridges and lighthouses, opened the Danube to steamer navigation, instituted the first official newspaper, and imposed sanitary measures to

Mahmud II, sultan of Turkey, 1808–1839. Engraving by John Young. *(Bibliothèque Nationale, Paris; Photo—Hachette)*

combat the plague. So far as the Balkan people were concerned, Mahmud's reforms were of less significance than might be expected. His great success was in asserting imperial authority by destroying the janissaries and such semi-independent local potentates as Ali Pasha of Albania. But this did not appreciably alter everyday life in the Balkans. The Ottoman officials remained, and they were as inefficient and corrupt as before. Appointments to provincial posts still were dependent on favoritism and bribery, and salaries still were discouragingly low. Nevertheless, Mahmud's assertion of central authority made possible further reforms in the following decades.

The great crises of 1831–1833 and 1839–1841, to which we now turn, reflect the inevitable clash between a strong sultan intent upon establishing his authority and an even stronger provincial pasha with far-reaching ambitions. Precisely how extensive were the ambitions of Mehemet Ali of Egypt is not entirely clear. Certainly he wished to gain control of the Arab provinces of the Ottoman Empire; perhaps he wished also to supplant the sultan and establish a new dynasty. In any case, either objective was bound to lead to war with the resolute Mahmud in Constantinople.

Like other pashas before him, Mehemet Ali first became master of his province, and then the weak central government recognized the *fait accompli.* There had been numerous such local potentates within the Ottoman Empire, and Mahmud was able to re-establish imperial authority over most of them. Against Mehemet Ali, however, he failed repeatedly, for that ruler differed fundamentally from other local chieftains. In the first place Egypt was much richer than other provinces, so that Mehemet Ali had abundant resources to draw upon. More important, Mehemet Ali was unique in realizing that the key to wealth and power was to be found in the West. Instead of squandering his revenues on personal pleasures, as did most other pashas, he built irrigation canals, constructed roads and ports, introduced cotton culture, and hired Western experts to organize a modern army and navy.

The net result was that Mehemet Ali became more powerful than his nominal master, Sultan Mahmud. Mehemet Ali used his forces to add the Sudan and part of the Arabian Peninsula to his domains. Then, as we have seen, he intervened in Greece after Mahmud promised to hand over Crete and the Peloponnesus. At Navarino he lost his fleet, but he did gain Crete as payment for his assistance.

From Greece, Mehemet Ali turned in 1831 to the rich province of Syria. It was this move that precipitated the showdown with Mahmud. Egyptian armies under Mehemet's son Ibrahim easily defeated the Turkish forces. They occupied Syria and then advanced across Asia Minor to Brusa, within striking distance of the Straits and Constantinople. The threat to the Ottoman capital at once involved the European powers. France favored the Egyptians. Mehemet Ali had primarily hired French experts to organize his armed forces; thus the more powerful Egypt became, the more influential France would be in the Near East. Russia, by contrast, was still following the policy laid down in 1829 at the time of the Adrianople treaty. She preferred to maintain the *status quo* with a weak Ottoman Empire rather than risk a change that might bring a strong rival into the Near East. This was essentially Britain's position also, but Britain at this time was too much involved in Belgium and Portugal to take action in the East.

Consequently, it was Russia that offered Mahmud a naval squadron for the protection of Constantinople. Mahmud accepted, and the squadron anchored before Constantinople, to the agitation of Britain and France. The immediate crisis passed when Mahmud finally agreed in the Convention of Kutahia (April 8, 1833) to cede to Mehemet Ali both Syria and the province of Adana in southwest Asia Minor.

This settlement merely papered over the cracks. Mahmud was determined to crush the upstart pasha and to recover his losses. He hired a young Prussian officer, Helmuth von Moltke, destined later to win fame as the victor at Sedan, to reorganize his armed forces. By 1839 Mahmud felt he was ready and gave the order to attack. This time the struggle was close, but Ibrahim again emerged the victor. Not only was the Turkish army defeated, but the newly built Turkish fleet sailed to Alexandria and surrendered to the Egyptians. It is not clear whether the Turkish admiral had been bribed to commit this extraordinary act or whether he had decided that the war was lost and that it was preferable to hand over the navy to the Muslim Egyptians than risk its fall to the infidel Russians.

Mahmud mercifully died just before news of this double disaster reached Constantinople. His successor, Abdul Mejid, was a boy of sixteen, lacking both ability and experience. He was rescued, however, by the energetic action of Lord Palmerston, the British foreign minister. Determined to save the Ottoman Empire and to curb the ambitious Egyptian pasha, Palmerston negotiated a program for common action with Austria, Prussia, and Russia. France sided with Mehemet Ali, and for a while there was danger of general war. In the end the French and Egyptians were obliged to give way before superior force. In 1841 Mehemet withdrew his forces completely from both Asia Minor and Syria, but in partial compensation he was allowed to keep the Sudan. He was also recognized by the sultan as the hereditary ruler of Egypt rather than as the mere pasha. Thus, although Mehemet Ali was prevented from becoming sultan or Arab emperor, he did found a dynasty that lasted until the dethronement of King Farouk in 1952.

Furthermore, these two crises had raised sharply the question of Ottoman integrity and had involved all the great powers more directly and unequivocally than at any time before.

Meanwhile, on November 3, 1839, young Sultan Abdul Mejid had issued a reform decree known as the Hatti Sherif of Gulhané. This decree stands out as the beginning of the reform movement commonly referred to as the Tanzimat, as it is called in Turkish. Mahmud had made the Tanzimat possible by establishing the authority of the central government. Now the Gulhané edict marked the beginning of actual legislation for reform. The edict set forth certain general objectives such as security for all subjects and regular procedures for army recruitment and for assessing and levying taxes. Mustafa Reshid Pasha, an enlightened bureaucrat, was the moving spirit behind the decree. During the 1840s he was responsible for a long series of specific reform measures designed to implement the Gulhané edict. Most of them did not pass beyond the paper stage, but there did remain a residue of real progress. The whole tone of life in the empire changed appreciably. The change was most noticeable in the sphere of law and general security. Arbitrary confiscation of property was becoming a thing of the past, as was also the use of torture to force confessions. Pashas could be brought to trial and punished for gross maladministration. Also Christians were now beginning to be recognized as equals with Moslems before the law, and their testimony was accepted in certain courts.

The Crimean War

In the midst of his struggle with Mehemet Ali, Palmerston explained the strategic considerations behind his diplomacy as follows:

Mehemet's real design is to establish an Arabian kingdom, including all the countries in which Arabic is the language. There might be no harm in such a thing in itself; but as it necessarily would imply the dismemberment of Turkey, we could not agree to it. Besides, Turkey is as good an occupier of the road to India as an active Arabian sovereign would be.[2]

These same considerations explain in large part the outbreak of the Crimean War in 1854. Palmerston again was in the British cabinet and he still believed that the preservation of the Ottoman Empire was essential for British imperial interests. In fact this conviction was strengthened by certain economic developments. Between 1825 and 1852, British exports to Turkey had jumped from £1,079,671 to £8,489,100, while in the same period, imports increased modestly from £1,207,172 to £2,252,283. Thus British exports to Turkey had increased eightfold, while imports had not even doubled. This left a favorable trade balance amounting to over £6,000,000 each year during the decade before the Crimean War. It is understandable that Palmerston should have informed the House of Commons in 1849 that: "If in a political point of view the independence of Turkey is of great importance, in a commercial sense it is of no less importance to this country. It is quite true that with no country is our trade so liberally permitted and carried on as with Turkey."[3]

British trade with India and the Far East also was booming, and this now was trade in bulky industrial commodities such as jute, rather than the spices, silks, and calicoes of earlier centuries. This created an increas-

[2] H. L. Bulwer, *The Life of . . . Viscount Palmerston* (London, 1870), II, 145.

[3] Cited by V. J. Puryear, *International Economics and Diplomacy in the Near East* (Stanford, 1935), p. 213.

ingly serious transportation problem, for the steamships now being introduced required so much coal and water for the long voyage around the Cape that little space was left for cargo. The solution was to return to the old Near Eastern trade routes that had been abandoned after Vasco da Gama's successful voyage around the Cape of Good Hope. The distance from England to India by way of the Suez was little more than one third of the Cape route. The precise manner in which the Near Eastern lands were to be traversed—by canal or railway or river transportation—had not yet been decided. But regardless of the method, the prerequisite was that the routes should not pass under the control of a rival great power. Thus British imperial strategy required that the Ottoman Empire be safeguarded against encroachment from any quarter.

These economic and strategic considerations alone do not explain the outbreak of the Crimean War. Equally important was blundering diplomacy, goaded on by inflamed public opinion. The Holy Places issue, which was the immediate cause for war, was an absurdly trivial "churchwardens' quarrel." The question was whether Greek Orthodox or Roman Catholic monks should control certain shrines in the Holy Land. Traditionally, Russia had supported the claims of the Orthodox monks and France the claims of the Catholic. During the wars and revolutionary disturbances of the late eighteenth and early nineteenth centuries, France was too preoccupied to pay attention to shrines in Palestine. The Greek monks, who continued to receive Russian backing, took advantage of the opportunity and gained control of various Holy Places originally held by the Latins. Suddenly this situation changed when Louis Napoleon came to power in France. In order to win the support of the powerful Catholic party, he demanded the reinstatement of the Latins in the Holy Places. After heavy pressure upon the sultan, in 1852 Napoleon did win back rights in several shrines for the Catholics.

Now began the series of blunders and misunderstandings that led ultimately to war. Public opinion in Russia was aroused by the concessions to the hated Latin heretics, so Tsar Nicholas sent Prince Menshikov to Constantinople to negotiate directly with the Turks. This was the first error, for Menshikov was a rough, overbearing soldier and, in addition, his instructions were impossible. He was not only to obtain full satisfaction concerning the Holy Places, but he was also to secure acknowledgment, embodied in a formal treaty, of the tsar's protectorate over all the Orthodox subjects of the sultan. The next step to war was the decision of the British government to send Stratford Canning as ambassador to Constantinople. A strong man with pronounced anti-Russian views, he played a key role during those prewireless years when a dispatch from London required over two weeks to reach Constantinople.

Stratford Canning arranged a settlement between the Turks and the Russians concerning the dispute over the Holy Places. Menshikov then proceeded, in accordance with his instructions, to demand a convention guaranteeing the ancient privileges of "the Orthodox Eastern religion, its clergy and possessions." Stratford Canning supported the Turks in rejecting this demand, pointing out that the term "religion" covered the sultan's twelve million Orthodox subjects, and that the proposed convention consequently infringed upon "the Integrity and Independence of the Ottoman Empire. . . ."[4] The Russians demanded acceptance of their proposal within eight days, and when this was again refused, they occupied the Danubian Principalities in July 1853. At the same time the British ordered their

[4] Cited by H. Temperley, *England and the Near East: The Crimea* (London, 1936), p. 321.

Mediterranean fleet to Besika Bay at the entrance of the Dardanelles. A day later the French fleet joined the British.

With Western fleets watching over the Russian army, war was now appreciably nearer. The task facing the diplomats was to find a formula that would assure the independence of Turkey, clear the Danubian Principalities of the Russians, and also save the face of the tsar. No less than eleven pacification projects were advanced during the second half of 1853, but they all came to naught. The difficulty was not only the *amour propre* of the Russians, but also the mounting war fever among the Turks. With the British and French fleets at Besika Bay, and assured of aid from the bey of Tunis and the khedive of Egypt, the Turks had no reason to be conciliatory. Thus when all the settlement proposals failed, the Turks issued on October 4 an ultimatum demanding the evacuation of the Danubian Principalities within fifteen days.

The Russians made no move, so the Turks sent raiding parties across the Danube and also a naval squadron into the Black Sea. The squadron was promptly wiped out by a superior Russian fleet at Sinope on the northern coast of Asia Minor. The "Sinope massacre," as it was unjustifiably called in England, aroused passions to such heights that general war became inevitable. Yielding to popular clamor, the British and French governments on February 27, 1854, sent an ultimatum to Russia demanding evacuation of the principalities. No reply was received, so the two Western powers declared war on March 28. Thus began a conflict that was unwanted by all the belligerents save the Turks. The roots of the Crimean War, therefore, may be traced to the background economic and strategic factors, to blundering diplomacy, and to inflamed public opinion.

Once the war began the belligerents faced the very

real problem of where to fight. Russia lacked the naval strength to invade the two Western countries. The latter did possess powerful fleets, but they could attack landlocked Russia only in two restricted areas, the Baltic and Black Sea coasts. They did make an attempt in the Baltic but were repelled by the guns of the Kronstadt fortress. The Allies also sent a joint force to the Bulgarian seaport of Varna, with the intention of marching north to the Danubian Principalities. But the Russians at this point evacuated the principalities because of an ultimatum from Austria. Rather than face still another enemy, the Tsar drew back his troops to his frontier.

Since the Allies had declared war in order to force this withdrawal, the object of their intervention appeared to have been attained. Yet the Allies now undertook a major operation by sending a joint expedition against the great Russian fortress of Sebastopol on the tip of the Crimea. The reason for this development was that the Western powers made a new demand: strict limitation of Russian naval armaments in the Black Sea. The Russians refused, so that a war that was precipitated by the question of the Danubian Principalities now was fought to the bitter end over the issue of Russian preponderance in the Black Sea.

The Crimean campaign is notable for the unpreparedness and incompetence of both belligerents. The supply and medical services were so inadquate that many more men died from lack of drugs and of health facilities than from enemy bullets. And this in an area that is a health resort in both summer and winter! The famous "Charge of the Light Brigade," immortalized by Tennyson's verse, symbolizes this war of blunders. As the British cavalrymen rode into the "valley of death," ringed by Russian cannon, a French officer remarked, *"C'est magnifique, mais ce n'est pas la guerre."* The ordeal finally was ended when the French managed to capture the Malakov strong point, a key sector of the Sebastopol fortress. The Russians then blew up their magazines, scuttled their fleet, and withdrew. On September 9, 1855, following a siege of 349 days, the Allies occupied the burning ruins of Sebastopol.

The loss of Sebastopol and the threat of Austrian intervention forced Russia to accept the Allied peace demands. The Treaty of Paris of March 30, 1856, included the following terms: the signatory powers guaranteed Ottoman independence and territorial integrity; the Black Sea was neutralized, with no fortifications on its coasts and no warships on its waters; and Russia regained Sebastopol but ceded southern Bessarabia to Moldavia, thereby losing access to the Danube.

In retrospect, the Crimean War had a greater impact on Europe than on the Balkans. It marked a turning point in the course of European diplomacy. In the first place, it tremendously enhanced the prestige of Napoleon and of France. The holding of the peace conference in Paris was symptomatic of the change in French fortunes. After 1856 France took the place of Austria as the leading power on the Continent.

More significant was the disruptive effect of the war upon the conservative, *status quo* bloc of the three Eastern powers, Russia, Prussia, and Austria. The effectiveness of this bloc had been demonstrated in 1849 when Tsar Nicholas sent an army to help the Hapsburg emperor crush the Hungarian rebels. Only a few years later, in 1854, Austria repaid Russia by delivering an ultimatum and aligning herself with Russia's enemies. This rupture between Russia and Austria was a diplomatic revolution of first-rate importance. The tripartite block no longer existed to maintain the *status quo.* Austria no longer could look to Russia or to Prussia for backing against the Western powers and against her own subject nationalities. Thus the Continent was unfrozen, and in little more than a decade Cavour unified Italy, Bismarck unified Germany, and Napoleon fell from the glory of the Malakov to the disaster of Sedan.

So far as the Balkans were concerned, the relevant provisions of the Treaty of Paris were soon violated by both Russia and the Allies. Russia repudiated the neutralization of the Black Sea in 1870, while Britain, Austria, and Russia all encroached on Ottoman integrity in 1878. Yet the Crimean War did significantly affect the course of Balkan history. It hastened the transformation of the Danubian Principalities into the united and independent Rumanian state. This outcome, though not anticipated by any of the belligerents, served to erect a substantial barrier to Russian expansionism.

C H A P T E R . . . 3

Winning of Independence 1856–1878

The significance of the period between 1856 and 1878 is that it witnessed the winning of independence by all the Balkan nationalities save the isolated and backward Albanians. When the Treaty of Paris was signed, its provision for the preservation of Ottoman integrity indicated indefinite continuation of Turkish rule over the Balkan Peninsula. At that time only a truncated Greece was independent and an equally truncated Serbia was autonomous. But within little more than two decades, the Rumanians and the Serbs were to win full legal independence, and the Bulgarians *de facto* independence. One reason for this outcome was the failure of a serious attempt that was made following the Crimean

War to improve the lot of the Balkan Christians. This failure ended what hope remained that the Balkan peoples could be persuaded to accept Ottoman rule rather than seeking national independence. In this chapter we shall consider first the failure of the reform effort and then the circumstances by which the various Balkan peoples freed themselves from the Turks.

Failure of Reform in the Balkans

A week before the signing of the Paris treaty the sultan issued the reform edict known as the Hatti-Humayun. This was the second Tanzimat or reform decree, following that of Gulhané promulgated in 1839. The powers officially took cognizance of the Hatti-Humayun by including a clause in the Paris treaty recognizing "the high value" of the edict and guaranteeing the integrity and independence of the Ottoman Empire. Thus the Turks were, at least in theory, given an opportunity to reform their empire without interference from the outside.

The first part of the Hatti-Humayun promised the non-Muslim groups of the empire equal rights in matters of taxation, justice, military service, education, public office, and social respect. These commitments were very difficult to implement; indeed, they proved to be impossible. The reason was partly the inefficiency and corruption of the Ottoman bureaucrats. But fully as responsible was the malfunctioning of the millet system. From the outset the theocratic Ottoman Empire had been organized on a religious rather than ethnic basis. The Turkish rulers had divided their subjects not into Greeks, Serbs, or Bulgarians, but rather into religious communities or millets, each with its own ecclesiastical leaders. The most privileged of these millets was the Orthodox, to which most of the Balkan Christians belonged, but in addition there were the Gregorian Armenian, Roman Catholic, Jewish, and Protestant millets. These religious communities had a very high degree of autonomy, so that the Christians were ruled, or misruled, as much by their own ecclesiastical leaders (and landowning primates) as by Ottoman bureaucrats.

This situation was made clear when, on June 11, 1860, the British ambassador in Constantinople circularized a questionnaire among his numerous consuls throughout the Ottoman Empire. One of his questions was: "Are many of the grievances of which the Christian population complains owing to the conduct of their own authorities?" The replies were invariably in the affirmative. Typical are the following reports from three of the consuls.

Consul Charles J. Calvert in Saloniki, July 23, 1860:

> The Christian authorities—by which I mean their Spiritual chiefs and their Primates ("Cojabashis")—are even more rapacious and tyrannical in their small sphere than the Turkish authorities are in a larger sphere. The Bishops and Metropolitans are guilty of many acts of oppression and cupidity towards their flocks, which, if committed by Turks, would arouse a storm of indignation on the part of the Christian sympathisers. Only a few days ago, the Bishop of Vodena, being in want of money, sent to a small hamlet of only forty families in his diocese and extorted 1000 piastres.[1]

Consul A. Cathcart in Prevesa, July 20, 1860:

> A vast deal of the discontent among the Christians arises from the petty exactions and tyranny of their own ecclesiastics, who exercise an almost unbounded authority. . . . Here,

[1] Great Britain, *Accounts and Papers. State Papers,* LXVII (1861), 3, 12.

as everywhere else in Turkey, every sort of injustice, malversation of funds, bribery, and corruption is openly attributed by the Christians to their clergy. The lower grades of priests who are miserably poor, are obliged to labor manually, and to dig and delve in the fields, like any other peasant, for a living, and are usually grossly ignorant; while the upper ranks roll in riches obtained from the vast unaudited funds of the Church, and are generally mixed up in every intrigue by which any money, influence, or position is to be obtained.[2]

Vice Consul Blunt in Adrianople, April 4, 1867:

These notables, be they Turks, Christians, or Jews, are, generally speaking, very despotic, and they take care to force the poorer classes, to pay much more than the richer, or to exact more than the legal amount. . . . The Greek Primates in this city levy a great deal more than the legal quota; the surplus falling almost exclusively on the poorer class. What they do with this surplus is a secret. They pretend that they employ it in support of the schools in this place. If this is true, Adrianople should have a greater number of schools and pupils than the other cities in the Vilayet, which is not the case. . . .[3]

The significance of the above testimony is that it demonstrates that the Balkan Christians suffered as much from the rapacity of their own ecclesiastical and civil leaders as from that of the Turks. In other words, reform was needed within the millets as well as in the empire as a whole. Reform decrees in Constantinople were of little use for the Christians so long as their relations with their own ruling class remained unchanged.

[2] *Ibid.*, p. 43.
[3] *Ibid.*, LXXV (1867), 34.

For this reason the Hatti-Humayun had provided specifically that the millets were to be reorganized to suit "the progress and enlightenment of the times."

Under Turkish prodding; and with the assistance of internal upheavals of laymen, the Orthodox, Armenian, and Jewish millets were in fact reformed during the 1860s. Provisions were made for greater lay participation in millet affairs, but this produced little improvement. The representatives who now shared in decision making came from the ruling elements, so that the basic problem remained unsolved. The same difficulty arose when in May 1856 the Turks began to allow Christian delegates to sit on the Imperial Grand Council composed of the ministers and dignitaries. Again the Christian representatives came from those families whose interests were identified with the *status quo*.

The Turks also sought to reform provincial administration by the vilayet law of 1864. This divided the empire into vilayets or provinces, which in turn were subdivided into sanjaks and other still smaller administrative units. These were to be administered with greater decentralization and popular participation than heretofore. The vilayet governors accordingly were given considerable authority, and they were assisted by new advisory bodies known as mejlisses. The latter's membership was partly appointed and partly elected by a complex indirect procedure.

One vilayet was set up in 1864 in Bulgaria to test the new law. The governor, Midhat Pasha, was of Pomak or Muslim Bulgarian origin. Being an exceptionally honest and energetic administrator, he transformed his vilayet into a showplace. He built roads, bridges, schools, and public buildings; established agrarian banks to lend to the peasants at low rates; and curbed brigandage to a large degree. These reforms won the enthusiastic support of both Christians and Muslims. But the governors who succeeded Midhat did not maintain his standards, and this was the case throughout the empire. Midhat unfortunately was an exception. Ottoman administrators generally were of poor caliber, so government in the vilayets remained correspondingly poor.

We may conclude that the serious efforts made after the Crimean War to introduce reforms in the Balkan lands met with little success. The Ottoman bureaucracy was unequal to the task, and the vested interests, both Muslim and Christian, were left largely untouched. This meant that the Balkan peasantry continued to suffer from insecurity and extortion. Hence Ottoman rule could not hope to counteract the centrifugal force of Balkan nationalism. The inevitable outcome was constantly growing nationalist movements that culminated eventually in independent Balkan nation states.

Making of Rumania

The first Balkan people to shake off Turkish control after the Crimean War were the Rumanians. These are the descendants of the original Dacian people, with additions of Roman, Slavic, and, to a much lesser degree, Tatar strains. These people occupy the lower Danubian lands on either side of the Transylvanian Alps. The "cisalpine" Rumanians live in the political entities of Moldavia, Wallachia, Bukovina, and Bessarabia, whereas the "transalpine" Rumanians occupy Transylvania and the Banat of Temesvar.

The original Dacians were under Roman rule between A.D. 100 and 275. When the Romans retreated to the southern bank of the Danube, the floodgates of invasion were left open. During the following centuries a host of barbarian invaders marched through the flat Rumanian valley lands on their way to the west and south. When this movement of peoples subsided, the

Rumanians were able to organize two semi-independent states, Wallachia and Moldavia, in the thirteenth and fourteenth centuries respectively. From the outset these states were in a precarious position, each being surrounded by powerful and aggressive neighbors. Wallachia had to contend with Turkey and Hungary, while Moldavia faced Turkey, Hungary, and Poland. When the Ottoman armies crushed all opposition in southeastern Europe, the Rumanians were forced to accept Turkish suzerainty. Wallachia became a Turkish dependency in the fifteenth century and Moldavia in the sixteenth. All the other Rumanian lands also fell to the Turks, so that when the Ottoman Empire was at its height it included both the "transalpine" and the "cisalpine" Rumanian people.

As the Ottoman Empire declined, it lost one Rumanian province after another to the neighboring powers. The Hapsburgs obtained Transylvania in 1699, the Banat of Temesvar in 1718, and Bukovina in 1775. Likewise Russia, having reached the Dniester River in 1792, annexed the province of Bessarabia in 1812. Thus by the nineteenth century only Moldavia and Wallachia were left to the Turks, and even here the sultan's authority was constantly being undermined. Probably, this was precisely the reason why these two principalities took the leadership in founding the new Rumanian state. Those Rumanians under the powerful Hapsburgs and Romanoffs had no opportunity for independent political action, whereas the ones under the tottering Ottomans could strike out on their own.

The Moldavian and Wallachian Rumanians enjoyed a certain measure of autonomy under the Turks, apart from the required payment of annual tribute to Constantinople. The great mass of the population, it should be emphasized, were serfs bound to the estates of Rumanian nobles or boyars. These boyars were the absolute masters of their serfs in very much the same manner as the Russian nobility of the period. The boyars also enjoyed the privilege of electing the ruling princes of the two principalities, who were known as hospodars. In actual practice the Turks took advantage of dissension among the boyars to influence directly and decisively the choice of hospodars. Aspirants to the princely offices had to bribe the sultan's ministers for their support. Before long the Turks were appointing and removing the hospodars in rapid succession, for the quicker the turnover the greater the proceeds. The net result was a system of economic exploitation and only nominal political autonomy.

Not at all nominal, however, was the steady Russian encroachment on the sultan's authority in Moldavia and Wallachia. The process began with the Russo-Turkish Treaty of Kuchuk Kainarji (1774), which enabled Russia to claim the right to protect the Christian religion and its churches throughout Turkey and also allowed the Russian ambassador in Constantinople to intercede in behalf of the Danubian Principalities. From then on the Russians steadily extended their authority in Moldavia and Wallachia until finally, with the Treaty of Adrianople in 1829, they became virtually corulers. This required that the sultan should accept the elected hospodars for life; he could not reject or dismiss them without Russia's concurrence; and he could not maintain any fortified place or any Muslim settlement anywhere in the principalities. The sultan also agreed that the Russians should occupy the two provinces until the last installment of the war indemnity had been paid. Finally, he undertook to accept the new constitution for the principalities which the Russian commander, General Kisselev, was preparing; and he even agreed that the Russian consuls in the principalities should be specifically authorized to watch over the working of the constitution. This gave the consuls a major role in Moldavian and Wallachian affairs. Indeed, the sultan ordered the hospodars to comply with the wishes of the consuls as much as possible. And it is known that some hospodars were dismissed and others appointed on Russian insistence. Thus the Adrianople treaty established a dual authority in the Danubian Principalities, and of the two powers Russia was clearly the senior partner.

We may conclude that in the early nineteenth century the outlook for the Rumanian people everywhere appeared dark and hopeless. Yet in 1848 they rebelled, as did the other subject nations of Europe, to make clear their desire for national unity and for independence. The uprising was a manifestation of the slowly developing nationalist movement among the Rumanians. But this movement was a narrow and rather esoteric affair. It was nationalistic but not national. It did not include the vast peasant mass that constituted the overwhelming majority of the Rumanian nation. These peasants were quite unaware of nationalism or constitutionalism or any of the other "isms" of the period. They were concerned only with land, servile dues, labor obligations, and other such matters that affected their daily lives.

But in addition to these inert peasants there was a small minority of intellectuals and of enlightened boyars who were very much influenced by various "isms" and who were the driving force behind the movement for independent Rumanian nationhood. The most important of the new intellectual currents were the so-called Latinist movement and, above all, the ideology and culture of France.

Latinism began in the late eighteenth century, when a number of Transylvanian Rumanians were sent to Jesuit institutions in Rome. The young students were inspired by the monuments of antiquity that they saw about them. The most exciting was the famous column of Trajan, the emperor who had made their own homeland, ancient Dacia, a part of the Roman Empire. It is not surprising that these young men, the representatives of a people who had suffered under foreign rule for centuries, responded enthusiastically to this association with a glorious past. They developed and popularized the theory that they were the direct descendants of the noble Romans. They claimed that the Rumanians were a chosen people, an outpost of Latin culture in the surrounding sea of Slavic and Teutonic barbarism. The chief work of these champions of Latinism was in the linguistic field. They substituted the Latin alphabet for the Slavonic which hitherto had been used. They purged the Rumanian language of Slavic, Greek, and other non-Latin words. They gradually secured the use of Rumanian as the language of instruction in place of the hitherto predominant Greek. These reforms helped to create a uniform literary language and thereby provided an essential basis for the development of Rumanian culture.

The influence of France was much greater than that of the shadowy Roman Empire. French ideas first reached the Rumanians by way of the Greeks, who at one time dominated the administration, the commerce, and the culture of the principalities. This was particularly true between 1711 and 1821 when the hospodars were selected from the ranks of the Greek Phanariotes. In addition to the Phanariotes there were droves of Greek merchants, clergymen, and teachers. Thus Bucharest and Jassy became, in the intellectual sense, as Greek as Athens and Janina. This meant that as Western secular thought penetrated the Greek world, it affected the politically conscious Rumanians as much as it did the Greeks. Furthermore, Rumanian students attended French universities in considerable numbers. Not all of them obtained their degrees, but they all returned ardent admirers of the great Latin sister nation. Their proudest boast was that their own Bucharest was the "Paris of the Balkans." Finally, the French Revolution and the exploits of Napoleon made a deep impression on politically minded Rumanians. The French vice-consul at Jassy reported: "For the small portion of the boyars who know how to reason, the French Revolution is not without attraction. They like to be told about it and cannot help showing a certain approval and at least admiring its prodigious accomplishments." [4]

Given this ideological background it is not surprising that Rumanian students took up arms when the 1848 revolutions swept over Europe. Some of the students participated in the February uprising in Paris, and then hurried home with rosy plans for the liberation of their countrymen. The uprising in the Moldavian capital, Jassy, proved a fiasco. It was poorly organized and the reigning hospodar was able to crush it quickly and easily. In Wallachia the revolutionaries were more successful. They organized street demonstrations and forced the hospodar to abdicate on June 25. Then they organized a provisional government, and proceeded to issue decrees abolishing ranks and establishing freedom of speech, assembly, and the press. The new government also declared itself for the unification of the Rumanian people. "All lands inhabited by Rumanians should be called Rumania and form one state . . . the Rumanian nation demands that it be one and indivisible."[5]

These dreams were soon dispelled by the facts of East European power politics. Russia insisted that the revolutionary regime near her border be destroyed. The Western countries were not sufficiently interested to support

[4] Cited by J. C. Campbell, "French Influence and the Rise of Roumanian Nationalism" (Harvard University, unpublished doctoral dissertation, 1940), p. 16.

[5] *Ibid.*, p. 210.

the provisional government against this pressure. Accordingly the sultan bowed to the will of the tsar. He sent an army across the Danube, and after a brief skirmish the provisional government collapsed and its leaders scattered in all directions.

Many of them fled to Paris where they sided with the republicans against Louis Napoleon. One of the Rumanians, Dimitrie Bratianu, was arrested and jailed for participating in a plot. While in prison he gave vent to his feelings in a letter in which he execrated Napoleon as "a bastard, a miserable wretch, without country and without family."[6] A few years later the same Bratianu gratefully hailed Napoleon as the founder of the Rumanian state. This tribute was fully deserved. Napoleon's foreign policy was based on support for Europe's subject nationalities. Napoleon therefore consistently and ardently urged that the principalities be united under a foreign prince.

Napoleon's chief opponent was Austria, partly because she had plans for the economic exploitation of the Rumanian lands, but primarily because she feared the attraction that a united Rumania would hold for her own Rumanian subjects in Transylvania and Bukovina. Turkey also opposed union, considering it with much justification as a long step toward full independence. Britain wavered from lukewarm acceptance of unification at the beginning to strong opposition before the end. Her traditional distrust of Russia explains the shift. Britain wanted to strengthen Turkey, and she feared that unification would soon deprive Turkey of her two strategic provinces across the Danube. The powers that backed Napoleon were Sardinia, who naturally favored the nationality principle, and Prussia, who desired to weaken her Austrian rival. But Napo-

[6] *Ibid.*, p. 360.

leon's chief ally, paradoxically enough, was Russia. By favoring unification Russia hoped to win the good will of the Rumanian people and also to widen the rift between Britain and France.

These differences among the powers came to the fore when the Rumanian question was raised at the Congress of Paris following the Crimean War. A final settlement could not be agreed upon, so a temporary compromise was arranged. The treaty provided that the wishes of the Rumanian people should be ascertained through freely elected assemblies representative of all classes in each principality. A commission, composed of representatives of the powers, was to meet in the principalities, determine the views of the assemblies, and report them to a future great-power conference that was to make the final decision. This procedure for consulting the people concerned was unimpeachably democratic. But in a land with mass illiteracy and despotic traditions it led to wholesale fraud and intimidation.

The first election was held in Moldavia on July 19, 1857. An antiunionist majority was returned, but only through the most blatant chicanery on the part of the Turkish-appointed officials. This precipitated an unseemly brawl among the representatives of the powers with Stratford Canning and the French ambassador, Thouvenel, in the forefront. Thouvenel, supported by the Russian, Prussian, and Sardinian representatives, presented to the Ottoman government what was in effect an ultimatum demanding the annulment of the election. Stratford Canning bristled and warned the Turks that if they did not stand firm the French ambassador "will ride roughshod over us."[7] The Turks refused to satisfy Thouvenel, who thereupon embarked dramatically on a French warship. The other three

[7] Cited by W. G. East, *The Union of Moldavia and Wallachia, 1859* (Cambridge, 1929), p. 104.

ministers broke off diplomatic relations at the same time.

The danger of war became real, and Palmerston increased it by informing the French ambassador in London that "the English were ready for any eventualities, however painful they may be."[8] Fortunately for the cause of peace, British public opinion was concentrated on the Indian Mutiny. This distraction left the more temperate elements in the cabinet free to restrain the bellicose Palmerston. By great good luck an official visit of Napoleon III and Empress Eugénie to Queen Victoria and Prince Albert had been arranged for August 6 at Osborne on the Isle of Wight. Long conversations between the sovereigns and their chief ministers finally produced a compromise. The elections were to be annulled, but in return Napoleon agreed that the Principalities should not be united. Instead, they were to receive "similar organic institutions" and "a common system in all things civil and military."

New elections were held in both principalities in September 1857. The assemblies met in Jassy and Bucharest the following month. They voted overwhelmingly that the principalities be united into a single state, subject to the suzerainty of the sultan, and under the constitutional government of a foreign prince. This was contrary to the terms of the agreement reached at Osborne. What were the powers to do? After months of deliberation they decided in the Paris convention of August 1858 that the principalities should remain separate, that each should have its own prince and its own parliament to be elected by itself, and that affairs common to both should be entrusted to a joint Central Commission of sixteen members consisting of an equal number of deputies from each parliament.

[8] Cited by T. W. Riker, *The Making of Roumania* (Oxford, 1931), p. 30.

This arrangement was artificial and clumsy, and failed to satisfy the aspirations of the Rumanian nationalists. But at least it placed them well along the road to unity. And their good fortune held out so that they quickly reached the end of the road. War clouds now were gathering over Europe. Events were under way that soon were to culminate in the Franco-Austrian war over Italy. While the powers were distracted by this crisis the Rumanians boldly cut the Gordian knot tied by the powers. The two parliaments met in their respective capitals in January and February 1859. Both unanimously elected as their prince the same man, a native boyar, Colonel Alexander Cuza.

Napoleon recognized Cuza at once. Austria and Turkey expressed strong opposition. Britain fortunately came forward with a face-saving formula that was accepted. Turkey recognized Cuza as prince with the understanding that this was an exceptional case and that the two separate parliaments should continue. Thus the "illegitimate offspring of the two Principalities," as a British consul called Cuza, was legitimatized. For all practical purposes a united and autonomous Rumanian state existed.

As prince of two principalities with two assemblies and two cabinets, Cuza spent half his time traveling back and forth between Bucharest and Jassy. Finally he persuaded the sultan to accept a real instead of a personal union of the principalities. On December 23, 1861, the union of the principalities was formally proclaimed. The new united and autonomous, though not independent, state was christened Rumania, with Bucharest as the capital.

Cuza ruled as prince until 1866, during which time he passed from one crisis to another. The basic reason was that Cuza was an ardent reformer who strove to improve the position of the downtrodden peasantry. This won him the irreconcilable opposition of the boyars, the only organized and articulate element in Rumanian society. Cuza lacked the demagogic qualities needed to arouse the active support of the peasants. Consequently the boyars were able, without opposition, to force Cuza to abdicate. He was succeeded by the Hohenzollern Prince Charles, a cousin of the king of Prussia. Charles was to remain on the throne until his death in 1914, and his descendants continued the dynasty until the Communist takeover after World War II.

Bulgarian Awakening

The Bulgarians were the first of the Balkan peoples to succumb to the Turkish invaders and, excepting the Albanians, the last to regain their independence. Their late awakening can be explained in large part by their location close to the center of Turkish power in Constantinople. One result of this proximity was that more Turks and other Muslim peoples settled in the Bulgarian lands than in the more distant Greek and Serbian provinces. Another result was that Turkish forces were able to reach the Bulgarian lands easily and quickly along the roads leading north and west from Constantinople. Finally, the location of the Bulgarians in the eastern part of the Balkans isolated them from the countries of Central and Western Europe. Unlike the Greeks, Serbians, and Rumanians, they did not have direct contact with any of the major powers of Europe. Thus the Bulgarians not only were subject more directly to Turkish power but also were deprived of the stimulating effects of Western contacts. Accordingly, they remained subject to Turkish domination longer than the other Balkan peoples who inhabited the more peripheral regions of the empire.

Turkish rule in Bulgaria, as in other parts of the

Balkans, was at first reasonably efficient and acceptable. But as the empire declined the Bulgarians, like their neighbors, suffered from the rise of chifliks and from the rapaciousness of Turkish bureaucrats and soldiers. In the late eighteenth and early nineteenth centuries the Bulgarian lands were particularly hard hit by the depredations of the kirjalis—armed bandits who roamed the countryside looting and devastating. Pasvan-Oglu was able to organize a popular and virtually independent regime at Vidin in the late eighteenth century precisely because he was strong enough to curb the depredations of both the kirjalis and the imperial officials.

In addition to the anarchy and extortion of Turkish rule, the unfortunate Bulgarians had to contend with economic and cultural exploitation by Greek prelates and teachers. Greeks monopolized all high church offices, which were regularly sold to the highest bidders. The sums expended for these offices were retrieved at the expense of the Bulgarian peasantry, and with enough margin to ensure rich profits. Greeks also controlled the schools and cultural life in general, though this was to a considerable degree unavoidable because of the cultural disparity between Greeks and Bulgarians. The latter were almost all illiterate peasants, wishing only to be left alone to earn their livelihood from the land, and caring little about either their past or their future. But as soon as some of them experienced a sense of national consciousness, they were bound to challenge the Greek hegemony. Thus the Bulgarian national awakening was as much anti-Greek as it was anti-Turkish.

The low point in Bulgarian fortunes was reached in the late eighteenth and early nineteenth centuries—the time when the Greeks and the Serbs were successfully struggling for freedom. Toward the middle of the nineteenth century, the Bulgarians began to show signs of national awakening. The rapid growth of commerce and handicrafts contributed much to this development. The economic revival was in large part stimulated by the substantial colonies of Bulgarians established abroad. The greatest of these was in Constantinople where, by the 1870s, some thirty or forty thousand Bulgarians worked and prospered as tailors, gardeners, and tradesmen. A few of them became immensely wealthy as contractors supplying cloth, foodstuffs, and other provisions to the Ottoman army and palace. Many Bulgarians also made their fortunes in Bucharest, Odessa, and other cities in Russia and the Danubian Principalities. Within Bulgaria itself handicrafts flourished in centers such as Gabrovo, Tirnovo, and Kotel. These, it should be noted, were all small and out-of-the-way mountain towns. They were preferred to large cities such as Sofia, Varna, and Ruschuk, which were located on the main routes and vulnerable to the disorders of the time.

This economic revival of the Bulgarians had cultural and political repercussions as far-reaching as that of the Greeks. The new class of merchants and moneyed men exerted a dynamic influence on Bulgarian society. Their contacts with the outside world had given them new ideas, while their wealth enabled them to act. They were particularly effective because of their organization into guilds. In these guilds they learned self-discipline and collective action. Each guild had its treasury, supported by dues, fines, and a profit tax. The large sums thus collected were used not only to meet the needs of the guild members but also to finance the work of national regeneration. It was the guilds that provided the new schools and books that were Bulgarian rather than Greek. It was their members who formed the bulk of the reading public which bought the books, newspapers, and journals. It was the guilds, also, that furnished most of the leaders of the nationalist movement. The Bulgarian national revival was to a very considerable degree the work of the Bulgarian guilds.

Foreign countries—especially Serbia, Greece, and Russia—also contributed to the national awakening. Bulgarian books were published in their presses, and Bulgarian students attended their schools. This was particularly true of Russia where, between 1856 and 1876, some five hundred Bulgarian students received scholarships for study. The Russians expected to indoctrinate the students with Pan-Slav, Orthodox ideas, but the outcome was very different. The Bulgarians instead came under the influence of Russian revolutionaries and returned home implacable opponents of both tsarist and Ottoman autocracy.

The first great victory for Bulgarian nationalism was the establishment in 1870 of a national church known as the exarchate. The origins of the movement for a national church go back to the 1820s when occasional demands were made for the rectification of financial abuses and for the appointment of Bulgarian bishops to head Bulgarian dioceses. Gradually the demands were raised until the Bulgarians were insisting on autonomy from the Greek-dominated patriarchate in Constantinople. This movement for a separate national church was political rather than religious in nature. It represented a clash of rival Greek and Bulgarian nationalisms rather than a dispute over religious doctrine. This became apparent when Patriarch Gregory VI offered in 1867 to accept an autonomous Bulgarian church on condition that its jurisdiction be limited to the territory between the Danube and the Balkan Mountains. Since church jurisdiction meant opportunity for political indoctrination, the Greeks drew the line at the Balkan Mountains in order to prevent Macedonia from falling to the Bulgarians. The latter, for precisely the same reason, rejected the patriarch's offer. Instead, they demanded that the population of all the dioceses should themselves decide to which church they should belong.

The deadlock was broken when the sultan on March 11, 1870 issued a firman establishing an autonomous Bulgarian church or exarchate. Its jurisdiction was limited to seventeen dioceses, but a key article provided that new dioceses could be added to the exarchate upon the vote of two thirds of the inhabitants. So far as the Bulgarian national revival was concerned, the establishment of the exarchate was a victory of incalculable importance. Patriarch Gregory VI had stated in 1867 that a Bulgarian church confined to the area north of the Balkan Mountains represented "a bridge to the political independence of the Bulgarians." Obviously a church that was free to expand anywhere it received a two-thirds majority was much more than a bridge. It was, in fact, a solid foundation for the independent Bulgarian state that now obviously could not be long forestalled.

The struggle against Greek ecclesiastical domination was paralleled by a struggle against Turkish political subjugation. At first the Bulgarian revolutionaries did not feel strong enough to make an independent bid for freedom. Instead, they supported other Balkan peoples when they rose in revolt. Many Bulgarians fought with the Serbs under Karageorge and Milosh Obrenovich. Many more joined the Philike Hetairia and fought in the Greek War of Independence. By the mid-nineteenth century the Bulgarian revolutionaries began to act for the liberation of their own country. As in the case of the other Balkan peoples, the attitudes of the various classes of the Bulgarian population varied a good deal. In the mountains there were the haiduk outlaws, the Bulgarian equivalent of the Greek klephts. They kept the spirit of resistance alive with their daring exploits, but they were few, unorganized, and ingenuous. Quite different were the chorbajis, corresponding to the Greek kodjabashis. These wealthy Bulgarians owned much land and also served as moneylenders and tax collectors. Because of their functions, these people were closely associated with, and dependent upon, the Ottoman imperial structure. Consequently they strongly opposed revolutionary action, though the more public-spirited of them supported peaceful reform. The peasants were generally passive, except in the northwest part of the country where chifliks were common.

The most militant of the leaders of the Bulgarian awakening came from the new class of craftsmen and merchants, including the teachers and writers who were dependent on them. Some of these people were reformers who worked for improved status within the Ottoman framework, while others were revolutionaries demanding nothing less than full independence. The Bulgarian communities abroad, which participated actively in the national movement, were also divided between revolution and reform. The large colony in Constantinople was predominantly reformist for understandable reasons. By contrast, the colony in Bucharest was largely revolutionary. The Rumanian capital was beyond the reach of the Turkish police, yet close enough for easy communications across the Danube. Thus it served as the center of numerous revolutionary groups which collected arms, hatched innumerable plots, and occasionally effected an actual revolt.

Under these circumstances a number of revolutionary leaders came to the fore—George Rakovski, Lyuben Karavelov, Vasil Levski, and Khristo Botev. To this day they are reverently referred to as the martyrs and the apostles. Their efforts were heroic but also tragic. They labored patiently in organizing secret conspiratorial groups, but more often than not they were betrayed.

When they were able to go so far as to actually take up arms, only a handful of supporters normally showed up. Revolution in the Bulgarian lands was much more difficult than in the more distant Greek and Serbian provinces. The net result of most uprisings was cruel retribution inflicted upon the innocent peasants living in the neighborhood involved.

As an example, a young revolutionary named George Benkovski planned a revolt for May 13, 1876. Because of treachery and arrests the revolt began instead on May 2 in the town of Panagyurishte in central Bulgaria. The rebels issued a proclamation that ended with these words: "From today on, we make known in the name of the Bulgarian people before all the world that we demand: Freedom or death to the people! Forward, forward, Brother, God is with us."[9] The excited populace assembled in the square, sang revolutionary songs, heard flaming speeches by Benkovski, and then scattered to kill Turkish settlers in the region.

The Ottoman authorities, alarmed by the violence of the outbreak, collected some 5000 regulars and also a considerable number of irregulars, the bashi-bazouks, recruited from the local population. Towns and villages fell one after another to these forces. The bashi-bazouks were particularly savage because of the earlier killings of their Muslim fellow villagers. When the looting and killing finally ended, thousands of bodies lay scattered among the ruins. An official Turkish estimate set the casualties at 3100 Christians and 400 Muslims. An American investigator estimated the dead at 15,000, while Bulgarian historians have claimed losses of 30,000 to 60,000.

This uprising was typical in its pattern, though the retribution inflicted by the Turks was exceptional. In

[9] Cited by A. Hajek, *Bulgarien unter den Türkenherrschaft* (Stuttgart, 1925), p. 262.

fact there was general revulsion in Russia and in Western Europe against the "Bulgarian Horrors," as they were promptly dubbed. The patriots had failed miserably as they had so often in the past. But their sacrifices this time were not in vain, for the "Horrors" helped to precipitate the intervention of the powers, which in turn led finally to the liberation of Bulgaria.

The Balkan Crisis and the Treaty of Berlin, 1878

Even before the perpetration of the "Bulgarian Horrors," the European powers had been aroused by an uprising against Turkish rule in the provinces of Bosnia and Herzegovina. The uprising, which occurred in the summer of 1875, was precipitated by various factors. One was the traditional antagonism between the Muslim landowning class and the Christian peasantry. Another was the pressure of extortionate tax farmers who persisted in collecting heavy levies despite crop failures. There were also provocations by local Austrian and Russian representatives, who encouraged the uprising often without, and even despite, orders from their superiors.

The Turks tried to placate the rebels with promises of reform, but to no avail. Similar promises had proved valueless in the past; the rebels now insisted on firm guarantees by the powers. The fighting raged on and became more widespread and savage. By March 1876, approximately 156,000 refugees from Bosnia and Herzegovina had crossed the frontiers into Serbia, Montenegro, and Austria-Hungary. Public opinion in Serbia and Montenegro was demanding intervention in behalf of the rebels who were fellow Slavs.

The spreading of the war, however, was strongly opposed by the three great powers of Central and Eastern

Europe—Austria-Hungary, Germany, and Russia. Since all three were then associated in the *Dreikaiserbund* or Three Emperors' League, their foreign ministers met in Berlin in May 1876 to work out a settlement. The outcome was the so-called Berlin Memorandum, which provided that the refugees be repatriated, that various reforms be introduced in the two provinces, and that the powers supervise both the repatriation and the implementation of the reforms.

This seemed to offer a promising way out, but an unexpected snag was hit when the British government flatly rejected the memorandum. The reason is to be found in the determination of the new British prime minister, Benjamin Disraeli, to follow a more aggressive foreign policy than had his pedecessor, William Gladstone. This explains why Disraeli purchased the Suez Canal shares of the khedive of Egypt in 1875, and in the following year proclaimed Queen Victoria "Empress of India." It was in keeping, then, that Disraeli should bristle when the *Dreikaiserbund* confronted him with the Berlin Memorandum in what he considered to be a highhanded manner. He had not been consulted in its preparation, and now he was asked to approve it within two days. Instead he rejected it, with the comment that Britain would not be treated as though she were a Montenegro or a Bosnia.

This action proved to be a turning point in the evolution of the crisis, because at about this time Serbia and Montenegro were being pushed into war and European public opinion was being aroused by the massacres in Bulgaria. In Serbia, Prince Milan was doing his best to restrain his bellicose subjects who clamored for intervention in behalf of their brethren across the frontier. But election results and popular demonstrations made it clear that if he did not accept war he would face revolution. Furthermore, the Russian consul, who was an ardent Pan-Slav, officially transmitted his government's earnest demand for peace but unofficially advised Milan to take up arms. On June 30, 1876, Milan gave way and proclaimed war against Turkey. He was immediately followed by Prince Nicholas of Montenegro. Since the two rulers were rivals for the leadership of the South Slavs, one could not remain inactive after the other had entered the fray. Thus Montenegrin troops invaded Herzegovina while the Serbs crossed over into Bosnia.

Meanwhile, eye-witness reports from Bulgaria revealed that well over ten thousand Christians had been massacred and several dozen villages destroyed. A storm of moral indignation swept over Europe, and especially England. The high point was Gladstone's passionate indictment of Turkish rule in his pamphlet, "Bulgarian Horrors and the Question of the East," of which it is said fifty thousand copies were sold in a few days. Gladstone did not call for outright partitioning of European Turkey. Rather, he demanded autonomy for the subject Christians so that they might be freed from the oppression of Turkish administrators and soldiers:

> Let the Turks now carry away their abuses in the only possible manner, namely by carrying off themselves. Their Zaptiehs and their Mudirs, their Bimbashis and their Yuzbachis, their Kaimakams and their Pashas, one and all, bag and baggage, shall, I hope, clear out from the province they have desolated and profaned.[10]

Disraeli, however, refused to bow to this popular clamor. He was convinced that the agitation was a momentary aberration, and he was determined to pursue a policy independent from that of the *Dreikaiserbund.*

[10] Cited by D. Harris, *Britain and the Bulgarian Horrors of 1876* (Chicago, 1939), p. 235.

A street scene in Turkey. *(Peace Corps Photo; Paul Conklin)*

Thus he defended the Turks as stoutly as Palmerston had done during the Crimean War. This led to increasingly strained relations with the Russian government, which also was under great public pressure for intervention in behalf of the fellow Slavs in the Balkans. The pressure increased when the Turks defeated the Serbs and drew near to Belgrade. Finally the tsar sent a forty-eight-hour ultimatum to Constantinople demanding an armistice of six weeks for the Serbs and Montenegrins. The Turks yielded and accepted the armistice on October 31, 1876.

This interlude provided the last opportunity for a peaceful settlement. The powers agreed to send representatives to a conference in Constantinople to work out terms. The British delegate was Lord Salisbury, one of the ministers who had less fear of Russia and more sympathy for the Balkan Christians than did Disraeli. Salisbury quickly reached an agreement with the Russian representative providing for a considerable degree of autonomy for both Bulgaria and Bosnia-Herzegovina. This plan was presented to the Turks as the "irreducible minimum" that the powers would accept. But Disraeli refused to back up his own representative. "Sal. seems most prejudiced," he wrote at this time, "and not to be aware, that his principal object, in being sent to Const., is to keep the Russians out of Turkey, not to create an ideal existence for Turkish Xtians."[11] The Turks, being aware of Disraeli's views, rejected the proposed settlement on the grounds that it violated the Treaty of Paris. Russia responded by declaring war on Turkey on April 24, 1877.

The Russian armies first marched through Rumania and then crossed the Danube and pushed rapidly southward to the Balkan Mountains. The farther the Rus-

[11] W. F. Monypenny and G. E. Buckle, *The Life of Benjamin Disraeli* (New York, 1920), VI, 111.

sians advanced the higher the tension mounted in Britain. The crisis then subsided for several months when the Russians were unexpectedly stalled before the Plevna fortress. Finally the Turkish garrison was starved out and forced to surrender on December 10. The Russians resumed their advance and by January 4, 1878, reached Sofia. The Turkish defenses now were crumbling. Armistice negotiations were opened, and on January 31 it was agreed that the Russian forces should occupy territory almost to the outskirts of Constantinople. Disraeli countered by ordering his fleet to enter the Straits, where it anchored on the Asiatic side of the Sea of Marmora. Thus less than fifty miles separated the Russian land forces from the British warships in the Straits. Peace hung in the balance in this precarious manner until, finally, the Turks and the Russians signed the Treaty of San Stefano, March 3, 1878.

The treaty provided that various reforms be introduced in Bosnia-Herzegovina, and that Serbia and Montenegro be made fully independent and somewhat enlarged. Rumania was also granted full independence and was to receive part of the Dobruja in return for southern Bessarabia, which went to Russia. Russia was to acquire, in lieu of the greater part of the financial indemnity that she claimed, Batum, Kars, Ardahan, and Bayazid in eastern Asia Minor. Bulgaria was to be established as an autonomous principality with an elected prince. The most significant provision of the treaty had to do with the territorial extent of the new principality. With the exception of Constantinople, Adrianople, and Saloniki, it included virtually all the territory between the Danube in the north, the Black Sea in the east, the Aegean Sea in the south, and Lake Ohrid and beyond in the west. Thus a greater Bulgaria was created and European Turkey virtually annihilated.

The San Stefano treaty aroused immediate opposition in almost all quarters. Both Britain and Austria-Hungary were convinced that the new Bulgarian principality would be merely a Russian outpost and would give Russia access to the Aegean and virtual control over Constantinople. Greece and Serbia also were opposed to San Stefano because it made Bulgaria the largest state in the Balkans. Particularly distasteful was the inclusion in Bulgaria of the disputed territory of Macedonia, whch was coveted by Greeks, Serbs, and Bulgars alike.

The Russians from the beginning had recognized the right of the other powers to pass upon those articles of the San Stefano treaty that infringed upon the 1856 settlement. They now agreed that a congress should be held in Berlin to reconsider those articles. But they did not anticipate the degree to which San Stefano was to be mutilated before the Treaty of Berlin was signed on July 13, 1878. The essential difference between the San Stefano and Berlin settlements had to do with Bulgaria. The large autonomous principality originally established now was divided into three parts: Bulgaria proper, north of the Balkan Mountains, to be autonomous with its own elected prince—though still tributary to Constantinople; Eastern Rumelia, south of the Balkan Mountains, to be under a Christian governor appointed by Constantinople but approved by the powers; and Macedonia, which was to remain under direct Turkish administration. Thus the Bulgaria of Berlin was only one third that of San Stefano and was completely cut off from the Aegean.

Serbia and Montenegro were declared independent and given additional territory. Rumania also became independent and acquired part of the Dobruja, though, as expected, she was forced to surrender southern Bessarabia to Russia. Bosnia and Herzegovina were handed over to Austria to occupy and administer but not to annex. Austria was also authorized to garrison the strategic Sanjak of Novibazar located between Serbia and Montenegro. This provision was designed to forestall a development that Austria always feared—a large, united Yugoslav state that might attract the South Slavs under Hapsburg rule. Greece claimed Crete, Thessaly, Epirus, and a part of Macedonia, but received nothing. The powers had so many other interests to promote that they evaded the Greek case by inviting the Turkish government to come to terms with Greece concerning the rectification of frontiers. Russia received Batum, Kars, and Ardahan in addition to southern Bessarabia. The British had prepared for this Russian advance in Asia Minor earlier by concluding, on June 4, the Cyprus Convention with the Turks. This committed the British to resist any further Russian expansion in Asia Minor; in return they were to occupy and administer the island of Cyprus for as long as the Russians retained Kars and Batum.

The Berlin treaty in one sense was a turning point, for it left all the Balkan peoples, excepting the Albanians, with independent or autonomous states. On the other hand, an essential feature of the treaty was its disregard of ethnic and nationalist considerations. Disraeli from the beginning made it clear that he was interested in checking Russia, and not, as he put it, in creating "an ideal existence for Turkish Xtians." As a result, every one of the Balkan peoples was left thoroughly dissatisfied. The Bulgarians were embittered by the partition of their country, the Serbians by the administrative advance of Austria into Bosnia-Herzegovina, the Rumanians by the loss of southern Bessarabia, and the Greeks by their failure to obtain any territorial compensation. This situation was particularly unfortunate because it provoked dissension and strife among the Balkan peoples. The establishment of the exarchate church had pitted Greek against Bulgar in Macedonia. Now, with Bosnia-Herzegovina all but formally in the hands of the Austrians, the Serbs also were forced to turn southward to Macedonia. The result was a suicidal three-cornered conflict that poisoned inter-Balkan relations and fomented anarchy and bloodshed in Macedonia until World War I and even later. For the Balkan peoples, then, the Treaty of Berlin meant frustration of national aspirations and future wars. The direct and logical outcome of the Berlin settlement was the Serbian-Bulgarian War of 1885, the Bosnian crisis of 1908, the two Balkan Wars of 1912–1913, and the murder of Archduke Francis Ferdinand in 1914.

C H A P T E R . . . 4

Age of Imperialism and Capitalism 1878–1914

The first three quarters of the nineteenth century constituted the revolutionary age of nationalism during which one autonomous and four independent Balkan states were established. The period from 1878 to 1914 proved to be an equally revolutionary age—the age of imperialism and capitalism, which, so far as the everyday life of the Balkan peoples was concerned, had deeper and more far-reaching repercussions than the age of nationalism.

This is not to say that nationalism played no role after 1878; it very much did so, and in certain respects in an even more spectacular fashion than ever before. But this did not represent something new. It was simply the continuation and completion of a movement that had begun a century earlier. What was new after 1878 was the rapidly increasing activity of the great powers and their all-pervasive impact upon the Balkans. This was manifested not only in the usual diplomatic channels but also, and most dramatically, in the economic realm. During these years the dynamic and expanding civilization of Western Europe impinged upon the Balkan Peninsula and undermined the latter's self-sufficient natural economy. This traditional economy gave way to a money or capitalist economy, which in turn led to fundamental changes in the social organization and daily life of the Balkan peoples. These manifold changes were not as spectacular and obtrusive as the various diplomatic crises and wars that punctuated this period. But for the daily life of the average Balkan peasant, the new imperialism and the new capitalism were infinitely more relevant and substantive.

The New Imperialism

It is well known that the end of the nineteenth century witnessed unprecedented colonial expansion on the part of the European powers. A combination of economic, political, and psychological factors led to the greatest land-grab in the history of the world, unequaled even by the conquests of Genghis Khan. Virtually all of Africa and parts of Asia were annexed outright by a handful of European states. Furthermore, their influence was not confined to the colonial territories that they owned outright; it also extended to other areas which were economically and militarily weak but which, for one reason or another, were not actually annexed. This was the case with the Ottoman Empire and the new Balkan succession states. Even though they did not suffer dismemberment, they did experience the disruptive impact of the new imperialism. They were subjected to intensive Western economic penetration, whose principal manifestations were government loans, which caused financial dependency, and railway building, which increased foreign indebtedness and also led directly to an influx of Western machine-made goods.

Government loans, railway building, and all the other modes of Western economic penetration in the Balkans started as early as the mid-nineteenth century at the time of the Crimean War. But in the late nineteenth century, under the pressure of the new imperialism, this penetration changed significantly in degree and in character. In degree, it became much more forceful and pervasive. Not only British and French but also Italian, Austrian, and especially German financiers appeared on the scene, all eager to gain a return on their money in excess of the 2 or 3 percent procurable at home. They invested their capital in unprecedented amounts, most of it being expended on military establishments and on railways, but some also being used to transform the Balkan scene with roads, ports, docks, tramways, irrigation works, and lighting and power plants. This was a far cry from the beginning of the century, when economic intercourse with the West was virtually limited to foreign ships calling at the seaports.

Western economic penetration also changed in character because of the growing tendency to identify private and national interests abroad. This identification meant, in practice, that private investors felt free to call on their governments to protect their foreign investments or to bring pressure to bear to make foreign investments possible. Conversely, the European governments encouraged loans to states considered friendly and discouraged loans to states deemed hostile. This development created a much more tense situation because considerations of national prestige now were introduced in a field hitherto regarded as beyond the realm of government concern. The appearance of this new imperialism, according to one authority, transformed the Balkans and the Middle East "from what had been regarded as a profitable field for investment and speculation into a cockpit of international rivalry."[1]

A brief over-all survey of railway building and of government loans will give a general impression of the new imperialism in practice. Railway building started in the Balkans after the Crimean War, when British interests built two lines from Constantsa and Varna on the Black Sea to Cernavoda and Ruschuk respectively, on the Danube. These were only local lines designed to enable the British to tap the commerce of the Danube valley. Preparations for large-scale construction began in 1868 when Sultan Abdul Aziz gave a concession for the building of a main stem to run from Constantinople through Adrianople, Philippopolis, Sofia, Nish, Sarajevo, and on to the Austrian border to connect with the Austrian southern railways and thence with Vienna. The concession was given to a certain Baron Hirsch, who was influential with the southern Austrian system. Construction did not begin till 1872, and by 1875, when the Near Eastern crisis intervened, the project was far from completed. Only two lines had been built: one from Saloniki to Üsküb and Mitrovitza, and the other from Constantinople to Adrianople and Sarambey in Eastern Rumelia, with a branch connecting this line with Dedeagach on the Aegean.

All these lines ran from the coastal ports into the Balkan interior, thus giving British commerce an opportunity to penetrate the peninsula. For this reason the

[1] D. C. Blaisdell, *European Financial Control in the Ottoman Empire* (New York, 1929), p. 217.

Austrian government was anxious to connect the Balkan railways with its own network. Specifically, it wished to see the Constantinople-Sarambey and Saloniki-Üsküb lines continued to Nish, whence Serbian lines could be built to Belgrade and on to Semlin on the Austrian border. For this reason the Treaty of Berlin included provisions requiring Bulgaria and Serbia to build the necessary connecting links running through their territories. This was done after many delays, and on August 12, 1888, the first through train rumbled over the tracks from Vienna to Constantinople.

During the following decades numerous proposals were advanced for additional railway construction. Very few went beyond the planning stage because of the conflicting political interests that were involved. Several chancellories scrutinized carefully every proposal for new track and did not hesitate to oppose it vigorously if their respective interests were not safeguarded. A good example was the rivalry between the Austrian interests that favored a north–south line through Bosnia and Novibazar to Saloniki, and the Serbian-Russian interests that wanted an east–west line between the Danube and the Adriatic. Proposals for such trans-Balkan lines were advanced periodically from the 1870s on. But Austria was determined to prevent Serbia and Russia from gaining access to the Adriatic through an east–west line, while Serbia in turn opposed a north-south line that would compete with her own railways and give Austria free access to the Aegean through purely Ottoman territory. The net result was that neither one of these trans-Balkan lines had been even started by the beginning of World War I.

Government loans were closely related to railway building as a means of Western economic penetration in the Balkans and in the rest of the Near East. Government loans, in fact, were necessitated by the heavy cost of railways as well as of other construction, such as roads and ports. Also, the burgeoning military and bureaucratic establishments contributed substantially to the growing indebtedness of the various governments. When the latter turned to the money markets for loans, the reception they received depended largely on political considerations, especially by the turn of the century. Bulgaria provides a good example of the manner in which foreign offices intervened in international financial transactions.

On March 13, 1912, Bulgaria signed an alliance with Serbia which became the cornerstone of the Russian-sponsored Balkan alliance system. Immediately thereafter Bulgaria turned to the Paris market for a substantial loan. An earlier application in 1909 had been turned down, but Bulgaria now had the backing of Russia. Therefore the French premier, Poincaré, who had opposed the original Bulgarian application for a loan, now reversed his position and gave his agreement in principle. But a few weeks later he returned to his earlier opposition, for King Ferdinand of Bulgaria had meanwhile visited Vienna and Berlin, where he was received with conspicuous honors. When the Balkan Wars ended in 1913, Bulgaria again sought a loan on the Paris market. The French government was still opposed, suspecting with justification that Ferdinand was drifting toward the Central Powers. But when Ferinand received some advances from Vienna banks, the French government became concerned and offered to support a loan if the Radoslavov cabinet were replaced by one less favorable to Germany. Now Germany in turn offered a loan on condition that a tobacco export monopoly be established under her control as security for the loan. France countered by dropping the condition concerning the Radoslavov cabinet, whereupon Germany waived her demand for loan security. Ferdinand finally accepted the German offer in 1914, a step that contributed to his decision the following year to join the Central Powers. Throughout this episode financial considerations were subordinated to political, and the loan was used as a pawn to attain diplomatic objectives.

Under these circumstances the Balkan states borrowed heavily on the European markets, so that, though they had negligible debts in 1878, they were all in serious financial difficulties by 1914. In the latter year the Bulgarian public debt amounted to 850 million francs, the Serbian 903 million francs, the Greek 1.25 billion francs, and the Rumanian 1.7 billion francs. Bulgaria was better off financially than most of her neighbors, yet by 1914 30 percent of her total government revenues was needed to service her debts. Finally, it should be noted that all the Balkan governments, with the exception of the Rumanian, had to accept arrangements whereby their creditors were given a measure of control over the revenues pledged to the payment of the bonds they held. In each case this foreign control was accepted to avoid bankruptcy or as a consequence of it.

The impact of the new imperialism upon the Balkans was much more profound than this brief survey would suggest. Thus far we have observed Western economic penetration from the outside. We have analyzed it in terms of loans and railways provided by the West. Now we shall reverse our procedure and look at the process from the inside. We shall examine the specific effects of Western economic penetration upon institutions and practices and everyday living within the peninsula. We shall note that the dynamic civilization of the West affected the Balkan peoples in myriad ways and operated as a powerful catalyst in stimulating the new capitalist order that was now appearing and that we shall next examine.

The New Capitalism

The Balkan peasants in the late nineteenth century were experiencing uncomfortably rapid change in virtually every field of life. Subsistence farming was giving way to commercial farming. Traditional customs were changing as communications between neighboring towns became more common. New political institutions were emerging with the rise of modern state structures of the Western type. What were the roots of these far-reaching changes and what was the general pattern of the new Balkans that finally took form?

One source of change was the winning of political independence by many of the Balkan peoples during the first three quarters of the nineteenth century. Those peasants who had been in feudal bondage now won their freedom, while many who had been landless were able to acquire plots. In general, political liberation created a more fluid social structure that was more susceptible to outside forces and to innovation. Political liberation also led to the appearance of the modern state, which took the place of the old feudal lord. The state was not as arbitrary as the lord had been, but it was fully as exacting, if not more so. The state rapidly created a large bureaucracy and army, which in turn involved heavy expenditures and a rising public debt. For the peasant this meant heavy taxes, burdensome service in the army, and periodic forced labor on roads and fortifications. In return for these burdens the peasant received very little from the state. Little wonder that he regarded this new impersonal master as something foreign and fearful. The hatred that he formerly held for the feudal lord he now turned against the bureaucrat, the tax collector, and the gendarme.

As significant as the appearance of modern state structures was the unprecedented increase of population in the Balkans during the nineteenth century. Greater security probably explains the growth of population in the early part of the century. The more rapid rate of increase after 1878 was caused by a fall in the death rate, usually explained by spreading medical knowledge and improved hygienic conditions. Thus the population of Serbia rose from 1.7 million in 1878 to 3.02 million in 1914, while that of Bulgaria, including Eastern Rumelia, increased from 2.82 million in 1881 to 4.33 million in 1911. Over a longer period the population of Moldavia and Wallachia rose from 1.5 million in 1815 to 7.2 million in 1912, and that of Greece increased from 750,000 in 1829 to 2,750,000 in 1912. Since the area of Greece during those years grew only slightly from 18,346 to 24,558 square miles, it follows that the population per square mile jumped from 41 to 114. This represents an almost threefold increase in less than a century.

The rapid growth of population had many important consequences. First, it compelled the Balkan peasantry to shift from a predominantly pastoral economy to an agricultural economy in order to increase their productivity. Instead of raising livestock, the average peasant now grew corn, grains, and potatoes in the interior of the peninsula and currants, tobacco, citrus fruit, olives, and grapes in the coastal Mediterranean areas. This shift to agriculture made possible the support of a much larger population than heretofore. Yet by the end of the century the soaring birth rate created a serious problem of agricultural overpopulation at the existing technological level. In Serbia the census of 1897 showed that over 11 percent of all rural households were landless. And this was in a country that had suffered from depopulation at the beginning of the century and that never had had large estates in any appreciable numbers.

In Rumania, where land distribution was less equitable, 60 percent of the peasants at the turn of the century either had no land at all or else owned less than seven acres.

This overpopulation had unhappy consequences for the Balkan peasants. The majority were landless or else owned tiny plots incapable of supporting their families. The situation steadily deteriorated because the constantly growing population led to progressive fragmentation of peasant properties. This land hunger in turn forced the prices of agricultural land to rise ever higher. In some areas the mounting pressures were relieved by large-scale emigration overseas. It is noteworthy that the heaviest emigration was from regions with poor soil, such as certain parts of Greece, or from regions where much of the land was held in large estates, such as Slavonia and the Voivodina. By contrast, there was comparatively light emigration from Serbia and Bulgaria, where land distribution was more equitable. Those regions that lost a large proportion of their young men do not seem to have experienced a labor shortage—an indication of the degree of their overpopulation. Rather, these regions experienced unprecedented prosperity because of the remittances of the industrious and thrifty emigrants. Greece represented the extreme case of a country whose entire national economy rested heavily on the golden flow of remittances from fabulous America.

The Balkan peasants were affected not only by the increase in their numbers but also by the steady, inexorable shift from the traditional natural economy to a money economy. Money had been used in the earlier economy but only in a peripheral manner. Production had been carried on by the peasant households primarily to satisfy family needs. A few commodities were sold in the local market, but not with the purpose of making profit. Rather the aim was to secure enough money to meet taxes and other obligations, as well as to buy a few essentials such as salt, a little iron, and perhaps a few pieces of cloth. In the latter part of the century this pattern changed radically. An increasing number of peasants began to produce primarily for the market in order to make a profit. In doing so they became dependent upon the growing market economy and fell subject to its all-pervading dynamics.

What persuaded the peasant to abandon his traditional manner of earning a livelihood? The truth is that he had little choice in the matter. The new economy was the product of forces that he could not control and that he probably did not comprehend. One was the building of railways, which had two direct effects. The money spent in the process of construction undermined the traditional self-sufficient economy of the regions immediately affected. Moreover, the railways, when completed, made possible the importation of large quantities of foreign machine-made goods. These goods were cheap and were bought to an increasing degree by the peasants, who thereby became correspondingly less self-sufficient.

Another factor responsible for the new money economy was the growing European demand for such Balkan agricultural products as Rumanian grain, Serbian livestock, and Greek currants and tobacco. Railway and steamship transportation now enabled the Balkan peasant to produce for the European market, and he did so to an increasing extent as the century progressed. If he had any hesitation about availing himself of the opportunity, he was soon forced to bestir himself by the growing demands of the tax collector. The new state apparatus, with its mushrooming bureaucracy and army, everywhere caused taxes to soar. This tax burden, together with the cost of the new manufactured goods now made available, compelled the peasant to earn a money income by increasing his production or by getting outside work or both.

This spread of the money economy had far-reaching social consequences, many of them uncomfortable and unsetting for the peasants. The manner of everyday living changed considerably. Tea, coffee, sugar, and similar commodities passed out of the class of luxury goods into more common use. Town-made lamps replaced the home-molded candles, and the more prosperous peasants also bought furniture and household utensils. Iron and steel plows became more common, though the poorer peasants still used the home-made ironshod variety. A few households bought some ready-made clothing, but the majority wove their garments from purchased yarn. In some peasant homes even a few books began to appear that were not exclusively religious. The number of purchased articles may appear insignificant by urban standards, but they represented, nevertheless, a radical departure from the self-sufficiency of earlier decades.

The diffusion of the money economy also increased village contacts with the outside world and thereby affected the traditional pattern of village life. The peasant sensed that literacy was essential under the new order if he were to be able to deal with the townsmen. Hence he readily accepted elementary schooling for his children whenever it was made available. Once reading and writing became reasonably common, new ideas and ethics, new tastes and ways of living, began to alter the age-old peasant traditions. The younger generation was soon questioning the assumptions and attitudes upon which peasant life had been based. Age no longer was regarded as sacrosanct. A new spirit of individualism and a desire for self-advancement and for personally owned possessions undermined the solidarity of village life and even of the family.

Village solidarity was also shattered by the development of economic stratification. The peasant was frequently unable to meet his obligations because he lacked the knowledge and the capital to increase his productivity and because opportunities for outside employment were scarce. As his debts mounted he was forced to turn to a new figure in the village—the well-to-do peasant who was turning merchant and moneylender. Being unfamiliar with money matters, the peasant frequently overburdened himself with debts at usurious rates ranging from 10 to over 100 percent. Peasant indebtedness early became a serious problem in each of the Balkan countries. The governments made some efforts to free the peasants from the usurers by providing credit at low rates. But the peasants usually were unable to provide the required security or else found the formalities and legal expenses excessive for the small sums they needed. Thus it was the usurers who borrowed the government funds at around 6 percent and reloaned them to the peasants at double, triple, or several times that rate.

Finally, the spread of the money economy made the Balkan peasants subject to the vagaries of the national, and even the international, market and credit mechanism. No sooner did they begin to produce for the European market than they felt the crushing competition of overseas agricultural products. The Balkan peasants by no means escaped the effects of the long depression that all European agriculture experienced from 1873 to the mid 1890s.

Purely national factors also affected the economic well-being of the Balkan peasants. Here, too, they felt helpless before something they could not control. That something they symbolized as the city. It was the city that was the center of political, commercial, industrial, and financial power. Try as they might, the peasants were unable to insulate themselves from its influence and control. The railway, the local usurer and storekeeper, the government-appointed teacher, tax-collector, and gendarme—all subjected the peasants to the new urban centers with inseverable bonds. The peasant reacted by turning against the omnipotent city and all that it stood for. This conflict was described by a Bulgarian novelist writing in 1892:

> The peasant has but the vaguest idea of our transition from servitude to independent life; for him it matters little whether he pays tax to Akhmed or Ivan. In fact, Ivan is often more distasteful to him than Akhmed, for Akhmed could be more easily fooled or bribed; Akhmed did not take his son off as a soldier whereas Ivan does; Akhmed was naïve and spoke Turkish, while Ivan is to all appearance a Christian like him, speaks Bulgarian, yet exacts more from him than did Akhmed. The meaning of state, rights, and duties for the peasant add up to tax-payment and sending his son off as a soldier. His attitude to nature, life and livelihood are still those of fifty years ago. [2]

In conclusion, we have seen that the transition from a natural to a money economy occurred because of the operation of domestic factors such as population increase and political change, and also because of the intrusion of the new imperialism with its loans and railways and machine-made goods and markets for Balkan raw materials. The end result was the emergence in the peninsula of what may be termed a new money economy or capitalist economy. This capitalism, needless to say, was quite different from the advanced industrial variety

[2] From Maksimov's novel, *Tselina* [Virgin Soil], cited by V. Pinto, "The Civil and Aesthetic Ideals of Bulgarian Narodnik Writers," *Slavonic and East European Review,* XXXII (June 1954), 357.

that prevailed in Western Europe. All the Balkan countries still remained overwhelmingly agrarian. Industries were few and were usually financed and operated by foreigners. Nevertheless, the new capitalism in the Balkans represented a fundamental break with the past. It affected profoundly not only the economies of the Balkan countries but also their political institutions and their traditional social patterns. Such disruptive change inevitably created a host of new problems—rural overpopulation, fragmentation of peasant properties, peasant indebtedness, and strife between the city and the village. These problems persisted not only to World War I but also to World War II, and even to the present day.

The Making of Bulgaria

In formulating his Balkan policy, Disraeli had assumed that a liberated Bulgaria would become a Russian tool. But soon after the establishment of autonomous Bulgaria, a British consul reported to London that there did not

> exist any Pan-Slavistic tendency, or even sympathy, among the Bulgarians, whether leaders or mass. Their tendencies are remarkably, I might almost say unamiably, exclusive; and may not incorrectly be defined as Pan-Bulgarian; nothing more. As to their Servian and Russian cousins, they make no secret of their hearty dislike of the former, and of their wish, gratitude apart, to be well rid of the latter.[3]

This "exclusiveness" became apparent when, in accordance with the Treaty of Berlin, an Assembly of Notables met at Tirnovo on February 22, 1879, in

[3] Cited by C. E. Black, *The Establishment of Constitutional Government in Bulgaria* (Princeton, 1943), p. 78.

order to prepare a constitution. The assembly, which was partly elected and partly appointed, soon crystallized into the Liberal and Conservative parties. This represented a continuation of the differences that had divided the Bulgarians under Turkish rule. During the struggle for ecclesiastical independence, the conservative Bulgarians had favored compromise with the patriarchate while the radicals had demanded a complete break and an autonomous church. Similarly, in the struggle against Turkish rule the conservatives had wanted reform while the radicals worked for revolution and independence. Now that the country had been liberated this cleavage persisted. The Conservative party leaders believed that their illiterate countrymen were not ready for democratic self-government and wanted political power entrusted to substantial citizens through an indirect system of voting or through a judiciously selected upper house. By contrast, the Liberals insisted on full popular sovereignty and opposed any artifice that limited the participation of citizens in government.

Since the Liberals dominated the Assembly of Notables, the constitution adopted on April 29, 1879, guaranteed civil liberties and delegated large powers to an assembly elected by universal suffrage. An attempt by the Conservatives to create an upper house was easily defeated.

The day after the constitution was adopted, Alexander of Battenberg was elected Prince of Bulgaria. In certain respects he was an ideal choice. He was a German prince, related by marriage to the English royal family, and a favorite nephew of the tsar. Furthermore, he had fought as a volunteer in the Russian army against the Turks, and was an attractive young man with a pleasant personality. These assets were more than neutralized, however, by a lack of experience and judgment. He regarded the Tirnovo constitution as "ridiculously liberal," and sought to transform his primitive peasant country into a strong military and aristocratic state of the type that he was familiar with in Germany. This attitude soon led to conflict with the Liberal party leaders, whose watchword was "the National Assembly makes the laws, the Prince proclaims them."[4]

The elections for the first Assembly, or Sobranie, were held on October 12, 1879, and the Liberals won a large majority. A deadlock ensued because Alexander had appointed a Conservative prime minister who now faced a preponderantly Liberal Assembly. Alexander finally ordered new elections for January 25, 1880, but again the Liberals won an overwhelming victory. The prince's position appeared to be hopeless. In desperation he appealed to Tsar Alexander II, with whom he had cordial personal relations. The tsar insisted that the Liberals be allowed to hold office in order to determine whether or not the constitution was a practical instrument of government. Accordingly, the Liberals formed a ministry on April 5, 1880, and remained in office one year.

Their record was, on the whole, creditable. They passed constructive legislation and were restrained and correct in their relations with Alexander. Yet Alexander remained convinced that his subjects looked to him rather than to the Liberal politicians, and that it was his duty to abolish the constitution that stood between himself and his people. The assassination of the tsar in March 1881 gave Prince Alexander the opportunity to have his way. The new tsar, Alexander III, was strongly opposed to liberalism and constitutionalism, so the prince took advantage of this situation to execute a coup on May 9, 1881. He dismissed the Liberal ministry and then held elections under conditions that, as the British consul reported, made the outcome a "foregone

[4] *Ibid.*, p. 119.

conclusion." The Liberal press was muzzled and uniformed officers at the polls openly questioned and intimidated the voters. The Assembly that met on July 31, 1881, was properly submissive. It unanimously accepted Alexander's demand that he be given extraordinary powers for seven years, and that at the end of that period the constitution be amended in the light of the experience acquired in the interim.

Paradoxically enough, Alexander's troubles henceforth increased rather than lessened. The basic difficulty was that neither Alexander nor the Conservatives had enough popular backing to rule the country without leaning upon Russia. Yet they were not willing to pay the price for this support. Russian contractors wanted to build a railway from the Danube to Sofia, while Russian speculators and concession-hunters regarded Bulgaria almost as a new imperial province opened for exploitation. But the Conservative leaders were unwilling to accept this semicolonial status and reserved lucrative investment openings for themselves and their friends. Thus Alexander and his associates were asking for both Russian protection and for full independence—two mutually exclusive conditions.

The outcome was a deadlock between the Russians on the one hand and Alexander and the Conservatives on the other. Relations became embittered as Russian officials disregarded Alexander and declared publicly that they were taking their orders from the tsar. In fact, Bulgarians of all political complexions reacted against these foreign taskmasters and wished above all else to be rid of them. Finally, after much negotiating and jockeying, Alexander and the two political parties of Bulgaria formed what was in effect a national front against the Russians. A new Liberal-Conservative coalition government took office and, on the insistence of the Liberals, the Tirnovo constitution was restored with the understanding that it would remain in force for three years before any amendments were considered. "The real common basis of this compromise," reported the Austrian consul, "is the prodigious hatred that has developed . . . of the Russian yoke which is becoming increasingly intolerable. . . . The program of the government may be summarized quite simply in the Italian formula: *La Bulgaria fara da se* [Bulgaria will do it herself]."[5]

Alexander took a momentous step in deciding to break with Russia. Apparently he assumed that the other powers would give him enough support to maintain his independent position. The assumption proved unjustified. The main reason was that the *Dreikaiserbund,* which had been shattered during the Balkan crisis of 1876–1878, was revived in 1881. Bismarck was determined that it should not founder again over another Balkan squabble, so he informed Prince Alexander with brutal frankness, "Germany has no interest in Bulgaria, our interest is: Peace with Russia. . . . if you wish to remain in Bulgaria . . . I advise you to seize any opportunity to restore good relations with Russia."[6]

Unfortunately for Prince Alexander, the course of events forced him to further defiance of Russia and soon afterwards to abdication. On September 18, 1885, an insurrection broke out in Eastern Rumelia, the Bulgarian-populated province that had been left under Turkish rule by the Berlin treaty. The rebels formed a provisional government and proclaimed the union of Eastern Rumelia with the principality of Bulgaria. This development was scarcely surprising since it had been common knowledge that the people of Eastern Rumelia

[5] *Ibid.,* pp. 238, 245.

[6] E. C. Corti, *Alexander von Battenberg: Sein Kampf mit den Zaren und Bismarck* (Vienna, 1920), pp. 165–168.

wanted unification. Nevertheless, this action represented a violation of the Treaty of Berlin; the great powers therefore held a conference in Constantinople in November 1885 to decide on what to do. In contrast to her position at the 1878 Berlin conference, Britain now favored unification. Since the Bulgarians had proven themselves quite independent of the Russians, Britain was now willing to accept an enlarged Bulgaria. Russia also was ready to go along with the union, but on condition that Alexander were removed from his throne in Sofia. To make her point clear, Russia recalled all her officers serving in Bulgaria. This virtually decapitated the Bulgarian army, all of whose officers above the rank of lieutenant had been Russians.

At this point, King Milan of Serbia laid violent hands on the course of events. He was determined to get territorial compensation to balance Bulgaria's sudden expansion southward. There was little hope of getting satisfaction through the powers, which were too divided for quick and concerted action. Accordingly, he invaded Bulgaria on November 13, 1885, expecting a quick victory over the disorganized Bulgarian army. Instead, his forces were defeated in the Battle of Slivnitza, and the triumphant Bulgarians then pushed deeply into Serbian territory. Milan was saved only by the intervention of Austria, which had concluded an alliance with Serbia in 1881. Austria now warned Prince Alexander to advance no farther, and on March 3, 1886, the Treaty of Bucharest was signed restoring the prewar *status quo.*

The victory of the Bulgarians ensured that the union of Eastern Rumelia and the Bulgarian Principality would not be undone. Even Russia recognized this fact and accepted a compromise arrangement providing for the personal union of the two areas. Because of Russia's insistence, Prince Alexander was not mentioned by name. Instead, the agreement reached on April 5, 1886, stipulated that the prince of Bulgaria be named governor of Eastern Rumelia for five years. Thus the violation of the Berlin treaty was concealed by this legal fig leaf.

The Russians had insisted that Alexander should not be specifically named the new governor of Eastern Rumelia because they were as determined as ever to drive him out of Bulgaria. On August 20, 1886, their wish was suddenly fulfilled when Alexander was melodramatically kidnapped in his palace and hustled across the border. The deed was not the work of a few hired miscreants, as is often claimed. Half of the regimental commanders and many higher officers participated in the plot. Some had decided that the unrelenting hostility of the tsar required that Alexander be removed for the good of the country. Others had personal grievances against Alexander involving promotions and discipline. Still others were dissatisfied with the terms of the personal union by which Alexander's legal status was virtually that of a Turkish pasha. In any case, the conspirators forced Alexander to sign papers of abdication, put him aboard his yacht, and landed him on Russian soil, where he was released.

The leaders of the revolt did not have definite plans as to what to do after Alexander had been removed. Also it soon became apparent that not all Bulgarians approved of the coup. The opposition elements were led by Stephen Stambulov, a bold and brilliant young politician of humble origin who earlier had attracted attention as a revolutionary against the Turks. He now organized a counterrevolution, scattered the rebel officers, and invited Prince Alexander to return. The latter did so, but Tsar Alexander made clear his wrathful opposition in a telegram that was virtually an ultimatum "Cannot approve your return to Bulgaria, foreseeing disastrous consequences to country already so severely tried. . . . Your Highness will judge what is your proper course."[7] The prince was overwhelmed by the tsar's relentless enmity and by the defection of his army officers. As the odds seemed impossible, he formally abdicated on September 7 and left Bulgaria.

Stambulov now was the real leader of the country. Despite contrary "advice" from the Russians, he held elections for a new Assembly on October 10, 1886. The returns gave Stambulov's National party an overwhelming majority. The first task of the new Assembly was to find a ruler. The fresh memory of what had happened to the previous prince scared off potential candidates. For six months the crown of Bulgaria went a-begging. Finally it was accepted by Prince Ferdinand of Saxe-Coburg. He estimated that he had a sporting chance to keep the crown on his head. "After all," he remarked, "if I am only the flea in the ear of the [Russian] bear, the experience ought to be none the less amusing."[8]

Stambulov was the natural choice to serve as premier under the new ruler. The ministry that he formed remained in office from September 1, 1887, to May 31, 1894. Despite this long tenure, Ferdinand and Stambulov were anything but compatible. Ferdinand was a proud, crafty, and inordinately ambitious aristocrat; Stambulov a talented but imperious and blunt-spoken plebeian. At first Ferdinand had no choice but to lean upon Stambulov, especially for unearthing numerous plots by Russian agents and their accomplices. But in 1894 Ferdinand suddenly dismissed his veteran premier. One reason was that Ferdinand wished to be ruler in fact as well as in name. Also, he felt able to take independ-

[7] A. H. Beaman, *M. Stambuloff* (London, 1895), p. 101.

[8] Cited by V. Chirol, *Fifty Years in a Changing World* (London, 1927), p. 129.

ent action because his position had been strengthened by his marriage to Princess Marie Louise of Parma and by the birth of a son and heir. This situation in turn made Ferdinand anxious to secure recognition from Russia in order to assure the future of his dynasty. But Stambulov was the leader of the anti-Russian forces in Bulgaria, and so long as he remained in office a *rapprochement* with Russia was out of the question.

Ferdinand not only dismissed Stambulov, he also persecuted him by sequestering most of his property and refusing him a passport to go abroad to recover his health. Stambulov characteristically retaliated with a violent personal diatribe in the press. Shortly thereafter, three assassins fell upon Stambulov in the street and beat him so savagely that he died three days later, on July 18, 1895. The police in the vicinity appeared unconcerned.

Ferdinand at last was the unchallenged master of his country. Immediately he took steps to end the rift with Russia. In addition to sending deputations to St. Petersburg, he rebaptized his son, Crown Prince Boris, in the Orthodox faith. Tsar Nicholas responded by standing as the godfather of the crown prince and sending a special envoy to represent him in the ceremonies held in February 1896. The tsar went further and took the initiative in procuring for Ferdinand the recognition of the great powers. The reconciliation between Russia and Bulgaria was complete, and Ferdinand at last had secured the recognition he had so long desired.

During the following decades, Ferdinand's rule in Bulgaria was based on two maxims: "Divide and rule" and "Every man has his price." As a result, Bulgaria soon had more political parties than any other country in the Balkans, and the labels of these parties signified little. The British historian R. W. Seton-Watson, who observed Bulgarian politics at this time, reported:

> The secret of Ferdinand's power has lain in his skill in calculating the psychological moment for driving each batch of swine from the trough of power. . . .There was always a waiting list for the post of Premier, and whenever Ferdinand had had enough of one politician and his following, he merely had to turn to a rival group and entrust it with the "making" of an election and a majority.[9]

From Ferdinand's viewpoint, this system proved eminently successful. He remained on his throne until 1918, when he was forced to abdicate for intervening in World War I on the side that lost the war.

The Macedonian Question

Ferdinand was ambitious concerning his position in the Balkans as well as in Bulgaria. An English journalist, to whom he granted an interview, found him standing before a window in a Napoleonic posture with one hand thrust in the breast of his tunic. "Do you see those mountains?" asked the prince, pointing to the south. "They are the key to Macedonia, and it is I who holds that key."[10] Ferdinand's melodramatic statement was not an empty one. After the unification of Bulgaria, the Macedonian issue became increasingly critical.

Macedonia may be defined as the area around Saloniki consisting roughly of the three Turkish vilayets of Saloniki, Monastir (Bitolj), and Kosovo. No other area in the Balkans has been the subject of so much dispute and the cause of so much bloodshed. To a very considerable degree Balkan diplomacy since 1878 has revolved around the explosive question of how Mace-

[9] R. W. Seton-Watson, *Europe in the Melting-Pot* (London, 1919), pp. 358, 360.

[10] R. Graves, *Storm Centres of the Near East* (London, 1933), p. 100.

donia should be divided among the three neighboring countries, Bulgaria, Greece, and Serbia.

One reason for the ruthless struggle for Macedonia is the strategic and economic value of the area. It commands the great corridor route that leads from Central Europe to the Mediterranean along the Morava and Vardar valleys, a route that has invited countless invaders, Roman, Gothic, Hun, Slav, and Turkish. Macedonia is also desirable because it includes the great port of Saloniki as well as the fertile plains much coveted in the mountainous Balkan Peninsula. As important as these strategic and economic considerations in explaining the struggle for Macedonia is the ethnic complexity of the area. The composition of this population provides all the neighboring countries with a basis for their aspirations and claims. Macedonia is a border zone where several ethnic blocs meet and overlap. It cannot be called a melting pot because intermarriage between the several ethnic elements has been rare. Individual villages and even various groups within a single village have retained their identity over periods of centuries. This freezing of ethnic strains explains the extraordinary assortment of peoples that have survived to the present day in an area about half the size of the state of New York.

Population statistics for Macedonia are virtually meaningless. Turkish authorities rarely bothered with a census, and when they did, the returns were computed on the basis of religious affiliation rather than language or nationality. Only a few general conclusions may safely be drawn from the available evidence. Those inhabitants of Macedonia who have lived close to the Greek, Bulgarian, and Serbian frontiers can be classified as being mostly Greek, Bulgarian, and Serbian, respectively. The remainder of the population, with the exception of such distinct minorities as Turks, Vlachs, Jews, and Albanians, may be considered as being distinctly Macedonian. These Macedonians have a dialect and certain cultural characteristics which justify their being classified as a distinct South Slav group.

The important point about these Macedonians, so far as Balkan politics were concerned, is that they lagged behind their neighbors in developing a sense of national consciousness. Accordingly, they were claimed by the Serbians, the Bulgarians, and the Greeks. The Serbians pointed to certain characteristics of their grammar and to their "slava" festival as proofs of their Serbian origin. The Bulgarians argued that physiologically the Macedonians were closer to them than to the Serbs and that the Macedonian language was in reality a Bulgarian dialect. Finally, the Greeks emphasized the fact that the Macedonians were Orthodox Christians and that many of them were under the jurisdiction of the patriarch of Constantinople. They also claimed that many Slav-speaking Macedonians considered themselves to be Greeks, and therefore they referred to them as Slavophone Greeks.

At the outset the Greeks had no competition in Macedonia, for the whole region was under the jurisdiction of the patriarch of Constantinople. This meant Greek education in the schools, Greek liturgy in the churches, and Greek prelates in all the higher ecclesiastical posts. Thus the Macedonians were subjected to an unchallenged process of Hellenization. In fact, they might well have become completely Hellenized were it not for the fact that they were almost all illiterate. The few who did acquire a formal education became Greeks to a greater or lesser extent. But the peasant masses of Macedonia were largely untouched by Greek culture in the academic sense and they continued to speak their Slavic dialects. This is significant, because so long as they retained their dialects and their customs they possessed the prerequisites for a national awakening in the future.

This situation changed drastically when the concept of nationalism reached the Balkans from the West and the newly established Balkan nation-states began to look covetously toward Macedonia. The Bulgarians, the first to challenge the hegemony of the Greeks in Macedonia, were to a large degree successful. Their instrument was the exarchate church established by Turkish firman in 1870. Under the terms of the firman the exarchate was limited almost entirely to the Bulgarian lands between the Danube and the Balkan Mountains. But Article X of the firman provided that additional territories might adhere to the new church if two thirds or more of the population so voted. This provided an entering wedge. By 1912 seven bishoprics in Macedonia had come under the jurisdiction of the exarchate. This in turn meant the replacing of Greek schools and teachers with Bulgarian. Indeed the Bulgarians themselves claimed that by 1895 they had some 600 to 700 schools in Macedonia with 25,000 to 30,000 pupils.

The fall of Stambulov in 1894 produced a change in Bulgarian tactics in Macedonia. Stambulov had followed a policy of peaceful penetration by cooperating with the Turks and receiving concessions in return. This procedure, though very effective, was undramatic and considered too slow. Even before Stambulov's downfall a number of Bulgarian Macedonians had gathered in the little Macedonian town of Resna in 1893 and established a secret revolutionary body known as the Internal Macedonian Revolutionary Organization, or IMRO. Its aim was to prepare the people of Macedonia for a great uprising against the Turks to gain their autonomy. The IMRO opposed the partitioning of Macedonia; instead, it favored a South Slav federation in which the Macedonians, together with the Bulgarians and Serbians, would participate. The IMRO was ably led and spread throughout Macedonia within a few years. Arms were gathered, men were trained, and plans made for a mass uprising.

In April 1895, a rival organization was established to foment revolution in Macedonia. This was known as the External Organization because it was founded outside Macedonia, in Sofia, and ostensibly represented the Macedonian immigrants in Bulgaria. It was organized under the auspices of the Bulgarian crown and was essentially a Bulgarian instrument, in contrast to the IMRO, which, at the outset at least, was a Macedonian movement. The slogan of the IMRO was "Macedonia for the Macedonians," but the External Organization wanted Macedonia for Bulgaria. The former body had more popular support within Macedonia, while the latter naturally was more favored in Sofia and received more backing there. The IMRO concentrated on organizing the population for a mass revolt and refrained from armed action until 1897, when it was forced to strike back after Turkish authorities uncovered a part of its underground network. The External Organization, on the other hand, resorted to violent measures from the outset, these usually taking the form of assassination or raiding parties across the frontier.

Macedonia, the Balkan States, and the Great Powers

The Bulgarian inroads into Macedonia naturally aroused both the Serbians and the Greeks. Before 1878 the Serbians had concentrated their attention on Bosnia-Herzegovina. But when Austria took over the administration of these two provinces, the Serbs were forced to turn to Macedonia. The Austrians encouraged them to do so by undertaking in the Austro-Serbian alliance of 1881 to help the Serbs expand southward. But it was not until the Serbs were defeated by the Bulgars in 1885 that they fully realized that Macedonia might follow the example of Eastern Rumelia and become a part of Bulgaria. The Serbs then took action and organized the Society of Saint Sava in 1886 with the purpose of stimulating nationalism in all Serbian lands and particularly in Macedonia. The society trained teachers, printed books, and conducted propaganda activities. The Turks welcomed the appearance of the Serbs in Macedonia and granted them various concessions in order to create a counterweight to the Bulgarians. By the mid-1890s the Serbs had established, according to their account, over 100 schools in the Kosovo vilayet with at least 5000 pupils. Serbia had become a force in the Macedonian embroglio.

The Greeks also took energetic measures to counter the Bulgarians in Macedonia. In November 1894, they founded in Athens a secret organization known as the Ethnike Hetairia, or National Society. It was supported by three quarters of the officers of the Greek army and by many wealthy and influential Greeks at home and abroad. Its ultimate aim was to liberate all Greeks under Turkish domination, but its immediate efforts were directed against the Bulgarian challenge. It subsidized Greek schools in Macedonia, and by 1895 these schools numbered, according to Greek statistics, over 1,400, with 80,000 pupils. The magnitude of this effort is indicated by the fact that the Greeks spent more money in proportion to population on schools in the so-called unredeemed territory than they did in Greece proper. The National Society also carried on propaganda work of a general nature and organized armed bands to make forays across the frontier.

The Serbians, Bulgarians, and Greeks were the main

contestants for Macedonia, but the Rumanians also attempted to stake out a claim. They based their case on the Vlachs, shepherds and traders who were widely scattered in Macedonia, Epirus, and Thessaly and who spoke a language akin to Rumanian. By 1912 the Rumanians were spending 1,000,000 francs a year in Macedonia for schools, which reputedly numbered over 30 with an enrollment of some 2000 pupils.

The over-all effect of this struggle for Macedonia was catastrophic, and the victims were the Macedonians themselves. This situation explains why the IMRO attracted so much popular support with its slogan of "Macedonia for the Macedonians." The miserable peasants were torn this way and that, and retribution was sure to follow whatever decision they made. If they declared for the exarchate, they could expect a visit from the Greek bands. If they remained under the patriarchate, they were hounded by the Bulgarians as traitors. And the Turkish troops that marched back and forth were almost as great a curse as the bands that they pursued but never banished.

One of the most discouraging features of the struggle for Macedonia was that it was self-perpetuating. It set one Balkan state against another and made it impossible for them to band together and to attempt a decisive settlement of the Macedonian problem. The Bulgarians were by no means solely responsible for the rivalry and disunity. In 1892 the Serbs and the Greeks tried to reach an agreement between themselves. Their purpose was to combat Bulgarian propaganda and, in their words, to "propagate the idea that there exist in Macedonia only Serbs and Greeks." But when they attempted to delimit their respective claims they discovered that they overlapped so extensively that an agreement was not feasible.

This discord among the Balkan states was fully

demonstrated during the Greco-Turkish War which began in April 1897 over the island of Crete. The people of the island, who were predominantly Greek Christians, had risen against Turkish rule virtually every decade during the nineteenth century. A revolution in 1896 aroused so much agitation on the Greek mainland that the Athens government was forced to intervene even though it was grossly unprepared. The Thirty Days' War that ensued was virtually a triumphal parade for the Turks. Thanks to the Macedonian issue, the Serbs and Bulgars stood by unconcerned as the Turkish armies marched through Thessaly toward Athens. Finally the powers intervened, if for no other reason than to save the Greek dynasty which was now intensely unpopular. By the peace treaty of December 4, 1897, the Turks returned almost all the Greek territory they had occupied and in return the Greeks paid an indemnity.

During these years the policies of Austria and Russia bore heavily on the Macedonian situation. The two powers concluded on May 8, 1897, the Goluchowski-Muraviev agreement with the professed purpose of "eliminating the danger of a rivalry disastrous to the peace of Europe on the seething soil of the Balkan Peninsula." The agreement provided that the *status quo* in the Balkans should be maintained as long as possible and that, if it could not be upheld, the two parties should cooperate to prevent any other power from acquiring territory in the peninsula. The significance of this agreement is apparent. The Austrians were concerned with domestic problems, while the Russians wished to be free to turn to the Far East. They therefore joined forces to "keep the Balkans on ice."

The determination of the neighboring great powers to freeze the *status quo* and the inability of the Balkan states to join for common action ensured the continuation of anarchy and bloodshed in Macedonia. In fact, the situation became steadily worse, particularly after November 1897, when the Turks uncovered a part of the IMRO underground organization. Up to that point the IMRO had concentrated on gathering arms and perfecting its organization. Now it was forced in self-defense to violent measures. This culminated in the IMRO uprising of August 1903. The rebels seized most of the Monastir vilayet, where they organized a revolutionary council and attempted to liberate the rest of Macedonia. Bands crossed over from Bulgaria and joined the insurgents. The Bulgarian government was taken by surprise and was far from pleased because it was not prepared for war. Yet it dared not close the border to the bands because popular sympathy for the insurgents was so strong that it feared an antidynastic movement. This was by no means farfetched because nearly half the population of Sofia at this time consisted of Macedonian refugees or immigrants. The Turks, meanwhile, were bringing up troops which, in customary fashion, indiscriminately harried the Macedonian peasantry with fire and sword. It is reported that some 200 villages and 12,000 houses were burned and 70,000 persons left homeless.

The revolt was quickly suppressed, but it did serve to goad the great powers to action. Austria and Russia, the two powers most immediately concerned, prepared the so-called Mürzsteg reform program of October 1903. It provided that a Russian and an Austrian civil agent should accompany the Turkish inspector general on his tours and report on conditions. The *gendarmerie* was to be reorganized and put under the command of a foreign general and a staff of foreign officers. In addition, the judicial system was to be reorganized and financial provisions made for the return of the refugees and for the rebuilding of houses and churches destroyed during the insurrection.

The other powers approved this reform plan, and the sultan thus felt constrained to accept it. But it contributed little to the pacificaion of Macedonia. In fact, it probably worsened the situation. A clause in the Mürzsteg program provided that when order was restored a new delimitation of administrative districts should be made along ethnic lines. This stimulated more propaganda and more violence as each side redoubled its efforts in order to improve its position in preparation for the day when the administrative boundaries were redrawn. More than ever before the Balkan states were deadlocked in their furious struggle for the control of Macedonia. Such was the situation in the Balkans when a totally unexpected event, the Young Turk revolt, suddenly changed the outlook completely.

The Young Turk Revolt

The autocratic ruler of the Ottoman Empire between 1876 and 1909 was Abdul Hamid II. He had come to the throne because of a liberal revolution organized by the reformer Midhat Pasha. Upon his accession, Abdul Hamid was required to accept a constitution providing for an elected parliament, a bill of rights, and an independent judiciary. Being determined, however, to be master of his empire, he had no intention of abiding by this constitution. First he dismissed Midhat Pasha from his position as grand vizir and banished him from Constantinople. Then when the first Turkish parliament met on March 8, 1877, Abdul Hamid used the outbreak of war with Russia as a pretext to adjourn meetings and to pack off the deputies to their respective constituencies. He never formally abolished the constitution, but parliament did not meet again until the revolution of 1908.

During his forty years of absolutist rule, Abdul Hamid had recurring trouble from two quarters. One was the national minorities, particularly those in Armenia, on the island of Crete, and in Macedonia. The other was his own Turkish subjects, and in the end it was they who brought about his downfall. From the 1860s, various liberal-minded Turkish critics of the Ottoman dynasty had been forced to flee abroad because of their opposition activities. Most of them congregated in Paris, where they continued their defiance and where they came to be known collectively as the Young Turks. Their numbers increased markedly during the Hamidian autocracy, and they included not only discontended Turks but also revolutionary leaders of the subject peoples. All these Ottoman exiles—Turks, Arabs, Greeks, Armenians, Albanians, Kurds, and Jews—held a congress in Paris in February 1902 with the aim of organizing a common front against Abdul Hamid. But they quickly discovered that they agreed on nothing except that they all disliked the sultan. One group, led by a veteran Young Turk, Ahmet Riza, stood for Turkish predominance and centralized rule, while another group, led by one of Abdul Hamid's relatives, Prince Sabah al-Din, favored a decentralized empire in which the subject people should have full autonomy.

While the exiled intellectuals were quarreling in Paris, Turkish army officers were taking decisive measures in Saloniki. One of the earliest leaders of these army officers was Mustafa Kemal, who was to win lasting fame after World War I as the founder of the Turkish Republic. In 1906 Kemal participated in the organization in Damascus of the secret military society Vatan, or Fatherland. This was later absorbed by another secret military organization, the Ottoman Society of Liberty, with headquarters in Saloniki. This organization spread throughout the empire very rapidly. Army officers were the backbone of the Society of Liberty, though they were greatly aided by other groups, and particularly by the Jews, who were the most numerous and wealthy element in Saloniki.

The Society of Liberty was organized into cells of five so that no one knew more than four fellow members. A new recruit had to be sponsored by a regular member and was observed closely during a probationary period. For the purpose of communication, each cell contained a "guide" who received the orders of the top central committee from the "guide" of another cell and who was required to pass on the orders without delay. There was a marked contrast between the rootless intellectuals arguing with each other in Paris and the practical revolutionaries quietly building up their underground organization within the empire. The latter group staged its revolt in July 1908, partly because the sultan's agents were beginning to penetrate its organization and also because the powers were openly considering intervention in Macedonia. In March 1908 the British foreign minister, Sir Edward Grey, proposed an autonomous regime for Macedonia. A little later it was announced that the British and Russian monarchs would meet at Reval on June 10 to discuss reforms for Macedonia. The Saloniki conspirators, fearing that the end result would be Ottoman partition, decided to act at once.

Events now moved quickly and according to plan. The Saloniki group telegraphed an ultimatum to the sultan threatening to march upon Constantinople unless the 1876 constitution was restored within twenty-four hours. The Third Army Corps solidly backed its revolutionary leaders. In Constantinople the State Council advised Abdul Hamid to comply with the ultimatum.

Also, the sheik ul Islam refused to issue a fetva authorizing suppression of the rebels. On July 24, Abdul Hamid proclaimed the restoration of the constitution.

The news of the sultan's capitulation was greeted with wild rejoicing. The long reign of repression was at an end. Christians and Turks embraced one another in the streets. The Young Turk leader Enver Pasha exclaimed: "There are no longer Bulgars, Greeks, Rumans, Jews, Mussulmans. We are all brothers beneath the same blue sky. We are all equal, we glory in being Ottoman."[11] This euphoric atmosphere did not last long. The issues that had divided the exiles in Paris now had to be faced as urgent issues of policy rather than differences in theory.

Three political groupings began to emerge at this point. The dominant one comprised the Saloniki leaders, now popularly known as the Young Turks. They were ready to grant political representation and religious freedom to all peoples of the empire on condition that they supported the empire and accepted Turkish predominance. The second group, the Liberal Union headed by Prince Sabah al-Din, held that only through local autonomy could the empire retain support of its peoples and thus survive. There is no way of knowing whether this proposition was sound because the Liberal Union lacked military power and remained an impotent opposition party. The third political group was the League of Mohammed. It demanded strict enforcement of the Sharia, or Sacred Law, and opposed the Saloniki Young Turks on the grounds that they were Westernized Turks who set a bad example by their irreligious ways. This argument was effective with the devout Muslim popu-

[11] Cited by H. Temperley, "British Policy towards Parliamentary Rule and Constitutionalism in Turkey (1830–1914)," *Cambridge Historical Journal,* IV (1932), 186.

lation, as the brief counterrevolution of 1909 was to demonstrate.

On April 12, 1909, an uprising in Constantinople upset the Young Turks and left the capital in the hands of conservative Muslim forces. Available evidence suggests that this was a spontaneous outbreak of the devout Muslim masses. The Young Turk leaders, however, assumed that Abdul Hamid was behind the counterrevolution. They accordingly gathered their forces in Macedonia, marched upon the capital, captured it after a few hours' fighting, and then compelled Abdul Hamid to abdicate. In his place they installed Mohammed V, a recluse who had spent his entire life in strict palace confinement and, according to his own account, had not been allowed to read a newspaper for ten years. The Young Turks therefore expected him to be a compliant figurehead. To make doubly sure, they revised the constitution so that the sultan was deprived of the power to dissolve parliament and the cabinet was made responsible to the parliament rather than to the sultan.

The Young Turks now were the unchallenged masters, and they proceeded with their policy of centralization and Turkish hegemony. They frequently stated that they wished all citizens of the empire to become Ottomans in the same manner that all citizens of France were Frenchmen. But this analogy was unrealistic. It failed to take into account the very different historical background and ethnic composition of Western Europe and the Near East. Genuine Ottoman nationality might have existed by the twentieth century if during the preceding centuries the Turks had not administered their empire on the millet principle and if, instead, they had coerced their subject peoples into becoming Muslims. But they had not taken these measures, and as a result their empire remained from beginning to end an aggregate of self-governing communities. Now it

Turkish recruits taken to the barracks during the Young Turk Revolt. *(Brown Brothers)*

was too late to attempt to fuse them into a homogeneous nation. The more they tried to do so the more opposition they aroused. Neither Turkish nationalism nor Ottoman nationalism could exorcise the inexorable awakening of Albanians, Arabs, Greeks, Bulgarians, and other peoples who still remained under Turkish rule. Indeed it was this futile campaign of the Young Turks that drove the Balkan countries to form the Balkan League and, at long last, to drive the Turks almost completely out of Europe. But before considering the Balkan League, we turn to the Bosnian crisis precipitated when the Austrian and Russian foreign ministers took advantage of the Young Turk revolution to fish in troubled Balkan waters.

The Bosnian Crisis

In the year 1906 Count Alois Aehrenthal and Alexander Izvolsky became the foreign ministers of Austria and Russia respectively. Both were capable, industrious, and extremely ambitious. They welcomed the Young Turk revolution as a diversion offering an opportunity to advance their fortunes. The two men met at Buchlau, in Moravia, where they agreed on September 16, 1908, that Russia would not oppose the annexation of Bosnia-Herzegovina by Austria and, in return, Austria would not oppose the opening of the Straits to Russian warships. But they did not set an exact date for the annexation of the two provinces, and this omission led to bitter controversy and a serious crisis.

Izvolsky assumed that nothing would be done immediately; he therefore began a leisurely tour of European capitals in order to obtain the consent of the powers to changes in the Straits regulations. Meanwhile, Aehrenthal was making the necessary arrangements for the annexation of Bosnia-Herzegovina. In order to be sure that Bulgaria would be on his side, he encouraged that country also to violate the Treaty of Berlin by proclaiming its independence from Turkey. The ambitious Ferdinand, who for years had been chafing under the limitations of Ottoman sovereignty, did not need further prompting. On October 5 he declared Bulgaria independent and assumed the proud title of tsar after the manner of the medieval Bulgarian kings. The next day, apparently by prearrangement, Aehrenthal announced the annexation of the two provinces by Austria.

These moves aroused a storm that brought Europe to the brink of war. The Serbians reacted perhaps the most violently against the incorporation of the two South Slav provinces into the Hapsburg empire. They had traditionally regarded Bosnia-Herzegovina as their rightful heritage. Now they refused to accept the Austrian annexation as final and raised the cry for revenge and restitution. In Russia also there was a strong popular reaction against the sacrifice of Slavic territory to the Hapsburgs. This feeling extended to the government, particularly because Izvolsky had not consulted his colleagues before concluding the Buchlau Agreement. Faced with this painful situation, Izvolsky tried to save himself by gaining some concessions at the Straits. Since neither his French nor British allies would support him on this matter, Izvolsky was forced to change his tactics and demand that the annexation of Bosnia-Herzegovina be submitted to a conference. Aehrenthal retorted that the annexation was a part of the Buchlau bargain and refused to accept a conference unless it met for the purpose of merely registering, rather than discussing, the annexation.

This controversy dragged on into the following year, with the Austrian and Russian foreign ministers accusing each other of lying about the agreement reached at

Buchlau. The situation was complicated by the demand of the Serbians that they should be given a portion of the disputed provinces as compensation. Izvolsky was compelled by Russian public opinion to support this demand, particularly because he had not been able to win any concession at the Straits. When Aehrenthal refused to hear of compensation, a complete deadlock ensued between Austria on the one side and Serbia and Russia on the other.

The outcome of the crisis was determined by the working of the European alliance system. Germany, being allied to Austria since 1879, backed her partner through thick and thin. On March 21, 1909, Izvolsky received a threatening note from Germany demanding whether or not he would accept the annexation. "We expect a precise answer—yes or no; we shall have to consider any evasive, conditional or unclear answer as a *refusal.* We should then draw back and let matters take their course; the responsibility for all subsequent events would then fall exclusively on M. Izvolsky."[12] The latter promptly gave the affirmative answer demanded. Serbia now was left alone and had no alternative to backing down. On March 31 she issued a note stating that her rights had not been affected by the *fait accompli* in Bosnia-Herzegovina and promising "to change the direction of her policy towards Austria-Hungary in order to live henceforth on terms of good neighborliness with the latter."[13]

It is clear in retrospect that the Bosnian crisis had most unfortunate consequences in the Balkans. It poisoned Austro-Serbian relations to the point where a peaceful settlement became virtually impossible. The crisis also ended the Austro-Russian cooperation that

[12] Cited by B. E. Schmitt, *The Annexation of Bosnia, 1908–1909* (Cambridge, 1937), p. 36, fn. 1.

[13] *Ibid.*, p. 216.

for some years had preserved a measure of balance in the Balkans. In place of cooperation the two powers henceforth engaged in what proved to be a mortal duel for influence in the peninsula. Russian diplomats worked energetically to organize a Balkan League that would serve as a barrier against Austria. Such a league was in fact founded in the spring of 1912. Thus the Balkan League and the Balkan Wars that followed may be said to stem directly from the crisis over Bosnia-Herzegovina. On October 2, 1912, when the Balkan Wars were about to begin, Count Berchtold, the Austrian foreign minister who succeeded Aehrenthal, wrote, "We delude ourselves if we do not face the fact that our procedure in annexing Bosnia and Herzegovina gave the first impetus to the Balkan League. . . ."[14]

The Balkan Wars

Two factors were primarily responsible for the organization of the Balkan League. One was the attempt of the Young Turks to enforce centralization and Turkish hegemony upon their polyglot empire. The other, and more important, factor was the reaction in Serbia and Russia to the Bosnian affair. In both countries it was felt that a Balkan bloc of some sort was needed to keep Austria in check. This feeling was shared by Russia's allies, Britain and France. The league did not actually materialize until four years after the Bosnian crisis. One reason for the delay was the ever-present Macedonian problem. Serbo-Bulgarian negotiations for an alliance in 1909 foundered on this issue. But then a strong stimulus for Balkan unity was provided by the outbreak of the Italo-Turkish War in September 1911,

[14] Berchtold memoir, October 2, 1912, in *Österreich-Ungarns Aussenpolitik von der bosnischen Krise 1908 bis zum Kriegsausbruch 1914*, IV, 528.

following the Italian invasion of Tripoli. This development encouraged Balkan statesmen to conclude alliance pacts in order to take advantage of Turkey's preoccupation.

Negotiations for a Serbo-Bulgarian alliance were pressed seriously after October 1911 with the energetic encouragement of the Russian minister in Belgrade. On March 13, 1912, the alliance was signed: the two states were to aid each other in case either was attacked and to take joint action against any great power which occupied any Balkan territory under Turkish suzerainty. This was obviously aimed at Austria. Two months later, on May 29, 1912, Greece and Bulgaria also concluded an alliance stipulating that if either of the signatories were attacked by Turkey, the other would give full aid. The last of these Balkan pacts were the alliances of Montenegro with Bulgaria and Serbia concluded in late September and on October 6, 1912, respectively. By this time the Balkan allies were definitely planning to attack Turkey; hence, these Montenegrin pacts were avowedly offensive in character. The Bulgaro-Montenegrin alliance required the signatories to begin hostilities against Turkey, Montenegro not later than September 20 and Bulgaria not later than one month after the Montenegrin action.

Russia's aim in encouraging and sponsoring the Balkan League was to use it as a weapon against Austria. Thus when the Balkan allies gave signs of acting independently and attacking Turkey on their own, the Russians tried to head them off. On October 8 Russia and Austria jointly warned the Balkan states that even if they defeated Turkey they would not be allowed to annex any territory. The warning came too late. On the same day Montenegro declared war on Turkey. Ten days later she was joined by her allies—Greece, Serbia, and Bulgaria. This denouement was characterized most aptly by the French premier, Raymond Poincaré, when he remarked, "it is too late to wipe out the movement which she [Russia] has called forth . . . she is trying to put on the brakes, but it is she who started the motor."[15]

The Balkan allies surprised all but a few well-informed experts by the rapidity and completeness of their victories. The Greeks drove northward, besieged Jannina and occupied Saloniki. The Serbs swept over the whole upper valley of the Vardar, the Sanjak of Novibazar, and the northern part of Albania, while the Montenegrins surrounded the fortress of Scutari. The Bulgarians invested Adrianople and hammered the main Turkish army back through Thrace to within a few miles of Constantinople. Jarred by these disasters, the Turks applied to the powers for mediation, and an armistice was concluded on December 3.

Some progress had been made toward negotiating a peace treaty when a *coup d'état* in Constantinople brought a more bellicose group into power. Thus the peace negotiations broke up in February and fighting was resumed. The Bulgarian army, reinforced by Serbian contingents, renewed its attack on Adrianople and entered the city on March 26. The Greeks successfully stormed Jannina on March 6, while the Montenegrins by April 22 had starved Scutari into submission. A new armistice was signed, with the Turks retaining nothing but Constantinople and its immediate environs. Finally, on May 30, 1913, the Treaty of London was signed by which the island of Crete and everything west of the Enez-Midye line were ceded to the allies.

With the Turks practically ousted from Europe, dissension now developed among the allies. The problem was how to divide the spoils. One complication arose from the fact that the great powers were insisting that

[15] Cited by S. B. Fay, *The Origins of the World War* (2nd ed., New York, 1934), I, 433.

an autonomous Albanian state be created from the wreckage of European Turkey. This meant that the Serbs would have to surrender to the new state some territory they had conquered. As compensation, the Serbs demanded portions of Macedonia claimed by the Bulgars. The latter indignantly rejected the Serbian demands, particularly because they had faced the largest Turkish armies and had done the heaviest fighting. There was also the question of the strategic Saloniki area, which had been occupied by the Greeks but which was also coveted by the Bulgars. Moreover, Rumania, as recompense for her neutrality, demanded a part of the Dobruja which had remained in the hands of Bulgaria after the Congress of Berlin. This question was arbitrated by a conference of the great powers and a very small boundary rectification finally was granted. Rumanian statesmen blamed Austria for the failure to obtain greater compensation and continued their hostility to Bulgaria.

The situation was further complicated by the conflicting policies of the powers. Russia, anxious to preserve the unity of the league, was concerned by the differences among the allies. The Belgrade and Sofia governments were reminded of a stipulation in the Serbo-Bulgarian Treaty providing for Russian arbitration in case of failure to attain agreement by direct negotiation. In contrast, Austria strove to disrupt the Balkan League by bringing Bulgaria and Rumania together. It is not surprising, under these circumstances, that the Balkan League foundered. On June 1, 1913, Greece and Serbia concluded an alliance directed against Bulgaria. The Russian government tried to arbitrate the issues in dispute but met with evasive replies.

At this point the Bulgarians made a fatal blunder. On the night of June 29–30 they attacked the Greek and Serbian lines in Macedonia. This seems to have

Area and Population of the Balkan States before and after the Balkan Wars*

	AREA (SQUARE MILES)			ESTIMATED POPULATION		
	Before	*After*	*Percent Change*	*Before*	*After*	*Percent Change*
Albania	....	11,317		....	850,000	
Bulgaria	33,647	43,310	+29	4,337,516	4,467,006	+ 3
Greece	25,014	41,933	+68	2,666,000	4,363,000	+ 67
Montenegro	3,474	5,603	+62	250,000	500,000	+100
Rumania	50,720	53,489	+ 5	7,230,418	7,516,418	+ 4
Serbia	16,650	33,891	+82	2,911,701	4,527,992	+ 55
Turkey in Europe	65,350	10,882	−83	6,130,200	1,891,000	− 69

* Source: *Report of the International Commission to Inquire into the Causes and Conduct of the Balkan Wars* (Washington, D. C., 1914), p. 418.

been intended as a means of strengthening Bulgaria's position in the settlement that appeared likely to come through the mediation of Russia. In other words, the advance was considered a political demonstration rather than a military measure. But the Serbians and the Greeks seized the opportunity and answered the Bulgarian "demonstration" with a declaration of war. Montenegro immediately joined Serbia against Bulgaria. On July 10 Rumania also declared war on Bulgaria. Two days later Turkey followed suit.

Attacked from all sides, Bulgaria was incapable of putting up serious resistance. Both Serbs and Greeks won easy victories. The Turks re-entered Adrianople and the Rumanians occupied the Dobruja. On July 31 an armistice was concluded, and on August 10 peace was signed by the Balkan states at Bucharest. Greece received Saloniki, Kavalla, and the greater part of the coast of Macedonia; Serbia was granted north and central Macedonia, including the city of Monastir (Bitolj); Rumania was allowed to keep a generous slice of the Dobruja; Montenegro extended her frontiers slightly until they touched Serbia; and Bulgaria retained only a small portion of Macedonia as the reward for her efforts during the first Balkan War. On September 29, Bulgaria and Turkey signed the Treaty of Constantinople by which Turkey regained the greater part of Thrace, including both Adrianople and Kirk-Kilissa. The territorial balance sheet at the end of the two Balkan Wars is summarized in the table opposite.

The effect of the Treaty of Bucharest on inter-Balkan relations is not difficult to surmise. The Balkan League was smashed. Bulgaria refused to accept the peace settlement as final. Greece, Serbia and Rumania were equally determined to preserve the *status quo*. This disunity was heightened by the great powers, and especially by

Austria and Russia, who pulled the Balkan states this way and that in their scramble for allies. Austria, for example, lured Bulgaria away from Russia and closer to the Central Powers. On the other hand, Russia developed cordial relations with Rumania despite an Austro-Rumanian alliance dating back to 1883. Greece at this time wavered between the two alliance camps, pulled toward one by British naval power in the Mediterranean and toward the other by a king who was married to the kaiser's sister. Serbia, of course, remained at odds with Austria and Bulgaria and was supplied with both loans and war materials by the Entente powers.

In conclusion, it is apparent that the Bucharest treaty settled nothing. It merely papered over the cracks for the time being. The period between the Balkan Wars and World War I was but a breathing spell during which the Balkan states jockeyed for position. With the coming of Sarajevo, each state stood ready to throw in its lot with whatever side seemed likely to satisfy its national ambitions. From the Balkan viewpoint, World War I was essentially a continuation of the Balkan Wars.

Sarajevo

On June 28, 1914, Archduke Francis Ferdinand, the heir to the Hapsburg throne, was assassinated at Sarajevo, the capital of Bosnia. The Vienna government sent a legal expert to the scene to collect evidence in order to prepare a tight case. In July 1914, the assassins were placed on trial and were found guilty. The verdict of the court included the following charge: "The Court regards it as proved by the evidence that both the *Narodna Odbrana* and military circles in the Kingdom of Serbia in charge of the espionage service, collaborated in the outrage. . . ."[16]

The Narodna Odbrana, or National Defense Society, which the court held responsible for the crime, had been organized in 1908, immediately following the Austrian annexation of Bosnia-Herzegovina. Indeed, so far as the immediate origins of the crime are concerned, the Bosnian crisis of 1908 is the obvious starting point. The Serbs never reconciled themselves to the loss of the two provinces, regarding them in the same light as the French did Alsace-Lorraine after 1871. Consequently the objectives of the Narodna Odbrana were avowedly revolutionary and anti-Austrian. It called for "encouragement and promotion of national feeling enrollment and recruitment of volunteers; formation of volunteer units and their training for armed activity."[17] Furthermore, the society enrolled recruits not only in Serbia but also in Croatia and Bosnia-Herzegovina. It is understandable, then, that the Austrians should have held this organization responsible for the assassination.

New evidence now available, however, indicates clearly that responsibility for the crime rests not with the Narodna Odbrana but rather with the secret Serbian organization, *Ujedinjenje ili Smrt* or Union or Death, more popularly known as the Black Hand. This was founded in Belgrade in 1911 with the aim of realizing "the national ideal: the union of all Serbs." The organizers were mostly army men who had played a prominent role in the murder in 1903 of King Alexander Obrenovich and the enthronement of Peter Karageorgevich. After that bloody episode they had become impatient with what they considered to be the dilatory

[16] Cited by L. Albertini, *The Origins of the War of 1914*, tr. and ed. by I. M. Massey (London, 1953), II, 68.
[17] *Ibid.*, I, 297.

tactics of the Serbian government and of the Narodna Odbrana. Their aim was to redeem their Serbian brothers under Hapsburg and Turkish rule by more violent and speedy measures. "This organization," the bylaws stated, "prefers terrorist action to intellectual propaganda, and for this reason must be kept absolutely secret from non-members."[18]

Before the Balkan Wars, the Black Hand had fought for the Serbian cause in Macedonia by conducting propaganda and organizing armed bands. It had also been active in Bosnia, where it operated through the Narodna Odbrana and other nationalist societies. The Black Hand infiltrated the older bodies, utilizing them to organize an underground revolutionary apparatus and to carry out assassinations. So effective was their work that a Serbian official described Bosnia at this time as a volcano that was about to erupt. "The year 1913 in Bosnia was the year of revolutionary organization. . . . 'Action, action, enough of words' was the cry on all lips. The young dreamed of nothing but bombs, assassinations, explosives to blow up and destroy everything."[19]

Although individual Serbian officials were involved in the Black Hand, the Serbian government, it should be noted, did not sponsor or support the organization. Rather the government was strongly opposed to it, partly because it was feared that the agitation might provoke Austria to attack Serbia. Indeed, the relations between the government and the Black Hand were anything but cordial. The secret organization operated almost as a state within a state, and Premier Nikola Pashich in Belgrade did not dare oppose it too openly for fear that he might meet the same fate as King Alexander in 1903.

[18] Cited by Fay, *op. cit.*, II, 87.
[19] Cited by Albertini, *op. cit.*, II, 21.

Archduke Francis Ferdinand and his wife about an hour before the assassination at Sarajevo. *(The Bettmann Archive)*

Such was the situation in Serbia and Bosnia when the announcement was made that Archduke Francis Ferdinand was to pay an official visit to Sarajevo on June 28. The decision was unpardonably shortsighted on many counts. The day selected was Vidovdan or St. Vitus' Day, commemorating the Battle of Kosovo, which in 1389 rang the death knell of the medieval Serbian empire. It was a day, therefore, when Serbian nationalist sentiment was bound to be inflamed. The decision was shortsighted also in view of the tense situation currently prevailing in Bosnia and the series of assassinations that had been perpetrated. Furthermore, the archduke was particularly hated by Serb nationalists because he favored transforming the Austro-Hungarian Empire from a dual to a triune empire. He proposed to do this by forming within the empire a third state consisting of the territories inhabited by the Croats, Slovenes, and Serbs. Such a state, he believed, would satisfy the nationalist aspirations of the South Slavs under Hapsburg rule and effectively neutralize Pan-Serb propaganda from Belgrade. The South Slav nationalists did, in fact, view this plan as a serious threat to their dream of a unified and independent Yugoslav state. It is ironical that Francis Ferdinand was killed by South Slav patriots precisely because he wished to raise the status of the South Slavs in the Dual Monarchy.

On June 28 the archduke and his duchess arrived for their official visit to the Bosnian capital. It was a radiant Sunday, and, by bitter coincidence, the anniversary of their marriage. At ten in the morning the procession of four cars entered the capital, proceeding in the direction of the city hall. No less than six Black Hand assassins were waiting along the route, armed with hand bombs and revolvers. Most of them lost their nerve at the critical moment or else were unable to act because the cars sped by too fast. But one of the assassins,

Nedeljko Chabrinovich, hurled a bomb that fell on the folded hood of the archduke's car. Thence it rolled off and exploded under the following car, wounding the archduke's adjutant.

The procession resumed its way, reduced to three cars. After the ceremonies at the city hall, Francis Ferdinand insisted on visiting his adjutant at the hospital. This involve a change of route, but the chauffeurs were not informed. The archduke's car consequently made a wrong turn. General Potiorek, the governor of Bosnia, who was in the back seat with the royal pair, leaned forward and ordered the chauffeur to stop, back, up, and turn to the right. This proved to be a fatal move. At that very corner was another revolutionary, Gavrilo Princip. He had let the car go past, but now that it had backed up in front of him he drew his revolver and fired two shots, one at Francis Ferdinand and the other at Potiorek. The second shot went wild and hit the duchess instead. Before medical aid arrived both the archduke and his wife were dead.

At the trial, held in July 1914, the defendants were defiant, and boldly stated their beliefs and motives. Princip, for example, declared:

> I have no regret because I am convinced that I have destroyed a scourge and done a good deed. . . . I have seen our people going steadily downhill. I am a peasant's son and know what is happening in the villages. . . . All this had its influence on me and also the fact of knowing that he [the archduke] was a German, an enemy of the Slavs. . . . As future Sovereign he would have prevented our union and carried out certain reforms which would have been clearly against our interests.[20]

[20] *Ibid.*, II, 49.

The teen-ager who so eloquently and resolutely defended his crime obviously did not foresee that it would lead directly to a world-wide war with terrible consequences. He could not have foreseen such an outcome because the war was not merely the product of the murder. Why should the whole world have taken up arms because of an assassination in an obscure Balkan provincial capital? Obviously other factors of general European origin were involved, including imperialism and the clash of rival alliance systems. It is by no means correct to state, as is done so often, that the Balkans were the "powder keg of Europe." It was all Europe that provided the powder for the keg.

Yet it cannot be denied that the Balkans did cause the spark that set off the fatal blast. This survey of Balkan history shows that the origin of the spark can be traced back to earlier centuries and developments—the evolution of the millet system in the theocratic Ottoman Empire, the lack of any sustained effort to convert the Balkan Christians to Islam, the gradual intrusion of the Western concepts of nationalism and the nation-state, and the role of these concepts in converting Macedonia into the cockpit of rival Balkan nationalisms. More immediately, there was Austria's annexation of Bosnia-Herzegovina, which envenomed Austro-Serbian relations to the point of no return and which ended Austro-Russian cooperation in the Balkans with shattering diplomatic repercussions. And in the background there was the ever-present despair of peasants beset by incomprehensible forces disrupting their daily lives—the despair voiced by Gavrilo Princip when he proclaimed before the court: "I am a peasant's son and know what is happening in the villages."

Bibliography

This bibliography includes only the outstanding works in the English language. A full bibliography of all sources is given in L. S. Stavrianos, ***The Balkans since 1453*** (New York, 1958).

The most detailed and recent general survey of Balkan history is the Stavrianos study, given above. An important inter-disciplinary analysis is provided by T. Stoianovich, ***A Study in Balkan Civilization*** (New York, 1967). For the period after World War I, see R. L. Wolff, ***The Balkans in Our Time*** (Cambridge, Mass., 1956), which covers the northern Balkans but not Greece. Interpretative essays on various aspects of modern Balkan history are provided in C. Jelavich, ed., ***The Balkans in Transition since the Eighteenth Century*** (Berkeley, 1963).

There are no good general accounts of Balkan geography and ethnography. Data on these subjects may be compiled from the relevant chapters in the ***Mid-European Studies Center Handbook Series, East Central Europe under the Communists*** (New York), the editors being R. F. Byrnes for ***Yugoslavia*** (1957); L. A. D. Dellin for ***Bulgaria*** (1957); S. Fischer-Galati for ***Romania*** (1957); and S. Skendi for ***Albania*** (1956). For Greece, see J. L. Myres, ***Geographical History in Greek Lands*** (New York, 1953).

Extremely interesting and significant studies of everyday life and of general social organization have been written by the following anthropologists: J. M. Halpern, ***A Serbian Village*** (New York, 1958); I. T. Sanders, ***Balkan Village***

don, 1962), being based on Bulgarian sources, though reflecting the viewpoint of current Bulgarian scholarship. See also C. E. Black, ***The Establishment of Constitutional Government in Bulgaria*** (Princeton, 1943).

The best account of the 1875–1878 crisis from the viewpoint of European diplomacy is the fine study by W. L. Langer, ***European Alliances and Alignments, 1871–1890*** (2d ed., New York, 1950). This work lists the large number of specialized studies of the crisis, including M. D. Stojanović, ***Great Powers and the Balkans, 1875–1878*** (Cambridge, 1878); G. H. Rupp, ***A Wavering Friendship: Russia and Austria, 1876–1878*** (Cambridge, Mass., 1941); B. H. Sumner, ***Russia and the Balkans, 1870–1880*** (Oxford, 1937); and R. W. Seton-Watson, ***Disraeli, Gladstone and the Eastern Question*** (London, 1935).

On imperialism and capitalism in the Balkans, see H. Feis, ***Europe, the World's Banker, 1870–1914*** (New Haven, 1930); D. Mitrany, ***Marx against the Peasant: A Study in Social Dogmatism*** (Chapel Hill, N. C., 1951); the articles by A. J. May on Balkan railways in the ***Journal of Modern History,*** December 1932 and December 1958; and especially the studies by various anthropologists listed above. Some of the reaction against imperialism and capitalism is evident in the following studies: W. O. McClellan, ***Svetozar Markovic and the Origins of Balkan Socialism*** (Princeton, 1964); J. Rothschild, ***The Communist Party of Bulgaria: Origins and Development, 1883–1936*** (New York, 1959); and L. Bushkoff, "Marxism, Communism and the Revolutionary Tradition in the Balkans, 1878–1924: An Analysis and an Interpretation," ***East European Quarterly,*** I (January 1968), 371–400.

On the making of Bulgaria, see the above works on Bulgaria and also C. Jelavich, ***Tsarist Russia and Balkan Nationalism*** (Berkeley, 1958); and W. N. Medlicott, "The Powers and the Unification of the Two Bulgarias, 1885," ***English Historical Review,*** January and April 1939.

There is no good, up-to-date study of the Macedonian question. See H. N. Brailsford, ***Macedonia: Its Races and their Future*** (London, 1906). The evolution of the Macedonian dispute is traced by H. R. Wilkinson, ***Maps and Politics: A Review of the Ethnographic Cartography of Macedonia*** (Liverpool, 1951). The effect of the Macedonian controversy on Balkan diplomacy is analyzed in L. S. Stavrianos, ***Balkan Federation: A History of the Movement toward Balkan Unity in Modern Times*** (Northampton, Mass., 1944), chaps. 6, 7.

Various aspects of the Young Turk revolt are presented in E. E. Ramsaur, Jr., ***The Young Turks: Prelude to the Revolution of 1908*** (Princeton, 1957); S. Mardin, ***The Genesis of Young Ottoman Thought*** (Princeton, 1962); B. Lewis, ***The Emergence of Modern Turkey*** (London, 1961); and J. Haslip, ***The Sultan: The Life of Abdul Hamid II*** (London, 1958).

The standard work on the Bosnian crisis is by B. E. Schmitt, ***The Annexation of Bosnia, 1908–1909*** (Cambridge, 1937); and on the Balkan Wars, E. C. Helmreich, ***The Diplomacy of the Balkan Wars, 1912–1913*** (Cambridge, Mass., 1938). Finally, the best and most recent analyses of the Sarajevo murder are in L. Albertini, ***The Origins of the War of 1914,*** tr. and ed. by I. M. Massey (London, 1953), vol. II, chaps. 1–3; and V. Dedijer, ***The Road to Sarajevo*** (London, 1967).

Index